◇ ◇ ◇ ◇ ◇ ◇ ◇ ◇ ◇

Crossing the Bridge

❖ ❖ ❖ ❖ ❖ ❖ ❖ ❖ ❖ ❖ ❖

Crossing the Bridge
A Jungian Approach to Adolescence

Kaspar Kiepenheuer

Translated by Karen R. Schneider

Open ❖ Court

La Salle, Illinois

THE REALITY OF THE PSYCHE SERIES

OPEN COURT and the above logo are registered in the U.S. Patent and Trademark Office.

©1990 by Open Court Publishing Company

First printing 1990

Printed and bound in the United States of America.

Library of Congress Cataloging-in-Publication Data

Kiepenheuer, Kaspar.
   [Geh über die Brücke. English]
   Crossing the bridge : a Jungian approach to adolescence / Kaspar Kiepenheuer ; translated by Karen R. Schneider.
      p.   cm. — (The Reality of the psyche series)
   Translation of: Geh über die Brücke.
   Includes bibliographical references and index.
   ISBN 0-8126-9136-9. — ISBN 0-8126-9137-7 (pbk.)
   1. Adolescent psychology. 2. Jung, C. G. (Carl Gustav), 1875–1961. 3. Adolescent psychology—Case studies.
4. Adolescent psychotherapy—Case studies. I. Title.
II. Series.
BF724.K5313   1990
155.5—dc20
                                      90-26888
                                        CIP

Contents

❖ ❖ ❖ ❖ ❖ ❖ ❖

Death and Rebirth in Adolescence

❖ ❖ ❖ ❖ ❖ ❖ ❖

Maria

❖ ❖ ❖ ❖ ❖ ❖ ❖

Martin

❖ ❖ ❖ ❖ ❖ ❖ ❖

Further Reflections on Childhood, Adolescence, and Death

❖ ❖ ❖ ❖ ❖ ❖ ❖

Illustrations

Foreword

It is with the greatest sense of privilege that I write these words to introduce the American edition of Dr. Kaspar Kiepenheuer's work on adolescence originally written in German and published in Switzerland. As colleague and friend, I have known of his work with children and adolescents for many years. In that work he combines unusual creativity and sensitivity with clinical knowledge and experience; humanity and compassion with clear insight into the problems which his young patients bring to him. He has provided, both in his own person and in the environment in which he works, an atmosphere which is itself healing.

I think of Dr. Kiepenheuer's workplace, where one passes through a beautiful garden to enter a space filled with creative options through which the stories of the adolescents can be expressed. High up in this place hangs a hammock, where the adolescents can choose to swing privately, protected, while they share with him their pain, their hopes, their fears, and their life expectations—a cocoon perhaps, which can hold them safely until they have passed through the profound transformation from childhood to adulthood.

These qualities of Dr. Kiepenheuer are clear in the moving descriptions of the lives of several adolescents which he shares in this volume. What is evident in this sharing is his awareness that the passage through adolescence is a natural and universal process which occurs within the psyche of every human being, regardless of outer circumstances of family and culture. And, just because it is a natural process within the psyche, there is an understanding that resources exist within the individual which can help restore the flow of movement in this process of growth, even in the face of great deprivation in outer life. Dr. Kiepenheuer articulates his respect for this internal process and trust in its potential healing in his description of the work with Maria, a girl of 17. "In the end, it was her dreams, and not the therapy, which gave her inner security and support. The therapy served only to help her relate to this inner world and to encourage her to stand up for it."

An understanding of the inner power of the psyche to heal itself and to support growth is a great source of inner hope. It also brings hope to the therapeutic process when applied to the general suffering of dark passages and despair. *Crossing the Bridge* is a moving and convincing document of this power of the psyche to heal, especially when supported by someone who believes in this source within the individual adolescent with both heart and mind. It is essential too that the therapist has had an experience of his own to ground his belief in such inner resources. Clearly this is true of Dr. Kiepenheuer, who is drawn into his own earlier inner passages through the work he describes.

That adolescents want to tell their stories is poignantly true. At a conference on youth suicide in Los Angeles in 1985, a speaker who worked for many years with suicide cases for the police department gave a single line of advice when the audience asked about prevention: "Listen and believe!"

In addition to his vision of the inner processes of the adolescent transition as natural and universal in the human psyche, the author clearly sees the impact of the larger context of family, community and contemporary culture upon the lives of the young people. Today, this larger context does not often support the transition of its adolescents. We often fail to understand the deep meaning of its emotional, physical and spiritual aspects. This lack is seen even more clearly in contrast to traditional cultures which honored this transformative time as a period of renewal and regeneration not only for the young persons, but for the community as a whole.

In his introduction and conclusion Dr. Kiepenheuer addresses the magnitude of the underlying discomfort and tension created by masses of youth dissatisfied in their transition into adulthood. He is acutely aware of the emergency solutions adopted by youth, in the absence of culturally supported transitions, solutions which in the United States have contributed to epidemics of suicide, tragedies of drugs and violence, and high rates of school dropouts and teenage pregnancies. I was recently in Africa working in a counselling center in a large metropolitan city. The adolescent problems in this urban area are of the same order as in the United States, and one feels the resulting tension of huge life energies, which are not being used for health and maturation, waiting to erupt. There, too, is a distancing from spiritual and cultural values which had previously supported life's transitions and strengthened the sense of community responsibility.

This book appears at a time in our history when the problems of youth are critical, not only for the young themselves, but for the future of civilization. To hear such a clear and passionate voice calling out for understanding of the pain and the deeply healing and creative potentialities within the young is an enormous source of hope for the adolescents themselves and their parents, as well as for all of us who remember our own adolescent transitions or are in similar periods of change.

When we recognize the naturalness and universality of the process of transition, we become aware that new light may come after a dark and difficult passage at any time in our lives. Recognizing this pattern in ourselves, we can then turn with understanding toward our collective responsibility to help our children over the bridge they must cross. I am personally deeply grateful for the inspiration this book provides for carrying out this essential task of human life.

Edith Sullwold
Founding Director,
Hilde Kirsch Children's Center
C.G. Jung Institute, Los Angeles

Death and Rebirth
in Adolescence

Adolescence as Transition

Writing about the critical life stage of adolescence is, for me, related to an entirely personal quest. It is, perhaps, an attempt to pick up again where I left childhood, indeed even to journey back over that bridge which separates me from childhood, to nourish myself once more in that 'paradise' and return with new vitality to shape and fulfill my life. This explains my burning interest in this threshold age. I believe that I could say nothing important about adolescence from a standpoint of serene detachment. I must be close to it, immersed in it, for my views to be valid. So much for motivation.

The motives of my readers may be different. Most of you have long since outgrown adolescence. Perhaps you find yourselves confronted with it anew through your own children. This time of breakthrough and transformation is familiar to you as adults through your own experience. Each of us looks back individually on this phase of life, and yet it is subject to universal, fundamental laws of human nature. Puberty seems to me therefore to offer a suitable model for a closer and deeper examination of the general process of human development and transformation. It appears to be a prototype for every crossroads in a person's life—marriage, giving birth, mid-life, death—and also for such life-changing experiences as loss, grief, and depression.

Transitions in life are times of the greatest danger, and puberty is especially so. The adolescent hangs, unprotected, in the vacuum created between the detachment from the intimate security of the earlier stage and the integration of the new one. In this way, too, adolescence is a precursor, a path-breaker, for transitions of every sort. The collective consciousness of mankind knows about such perils. Carefully handed-down rites provide for appropriate protection during the most important transitions in life. Baptism, marriage, and burial rituals escort the participant 'across' the passage, and provide a time for reflection when shared values, which otherwise have no place in the routine of everyday living, can be celebrated.*

Only puberty seems in this regard to have become a stepchild, at least in our culture. The dangers lying along the road of transition become especially clear at the time of puberty. A good many young people crash into the drug world, or do violence to themselves in other irreparable ways. The inner conflicts of adolescence, and the weakened sense of reality which accompanies them, can also form the basis for the outbreak of a first phase of schizophrenia. Indeed, one might even say that puberty is a more or less mild form of transient schizophrenia.

As experiences take on a fluidity, one connects to what has been forgotten, to the primal experiences of one's personal life-history, but beyond this, to the collective experiences of human history. Forgotten, dormant powers come into play. It is as if one 'remembers' things never known before, similar to other times of physical and emotional crisis. These are border experiences, in which powers liberated from among one's own resources can serve both to overcome the crisis and to pave the way for new growth. Certainly, this perspective is not apparent in the crush of the crisis itself. And perhaps the direction of development even turns momentarily back, into a protective regression. This should not be viewed judgementally as a retreat, but rather as a step backward in preparation for a more determined move forward.

---

*'Puberty' refers to a precise stage in the biological development of a young person. 'Adolescence', which covers a longer age span, refers to the transient period between puberty and adulthood. In traditional societies, rites for girls were often precisely timed, sometimes at the time of first menstruation, as among the Navaho, while so-called puberty rites for boys were often not performed until they were psychologically more ready. See *Betwixt and Between: Patterns of Masculine and Feminine Initiation*, edited by Louise Carus Mahdi, with Steven Foster and Meredith Little (Open Court: 1987).

Outer Events

Puberty is a revolution, above all because of the radical physical changes which take place in this time of growing up. The young man or woman is, so to speak, cast out of his or her familiar skin. The changes begin in girls already around the age of twelve, in boys later, at approximately 14. The upper limit where adolescence ends and adulthood begins is much more fluid. These young people appear divided against themselves. Physically they are full of contradictions, and the various developmental aspects can diverge widely. On the one hand they may be nearly sexually mature, yet on the other, they remain childish, playful, and innocent. Sometimes they feel that others look at them strangely because they are no longer 'the same sweet child.' They feel that they have been thrown out of childhood without having reached the new status of adult. Because they now have the outward characteristics of grown-ups, they sense that others expect more from them. Sexual stirrings come from within, but are also heralded from without. This arouses curiosity and fear at the same time.

Adolescents feel that they have been banished from parental security, even if they themselves wanted, and perhaps even provoked, the separation. They have outgrown their cozy home, only to be faced with a world and an environment which man himself has placed in the greatest danger. This gives rise to concrete, legitimate fears, but is also the starting point for inner patterns of anxiety, which can be projected widely. In teenagers, fantasies of world conquest alternate with fear of their personal future, and boundless overestimation of themselves vies with pathetic helplessness and dread of the world into which they find themselves suddenly thrown. They may look for caring support from their parents, then in turn push them abruptly aside in their search for freedom and personal identity. Now they admire adults as the embodiment of an ideal, as idols, now they reject them with moral indignation. They may devote themselves to lofty principles, then stress sober objectivity, be exhilarated one minute and down in the dumps the next, all without knowing why.

They are 'neither fish nor fowl', as the folk saying goes, belonging neither to water nor to air, or, if one interprets these elements symbolically, established neither in the unconscious nor in spiritual consciousness. Adolescents are suspended between the worlds: no longer child, not yet man or woman; half member of the family, half member of a larger society; partly bound to the mother, partly turned toward the realm of the father; needing protective mother-love, but simultaneously experiencing it as dangerous and devouring; actively seeking the father and at the same time fearing and fighting him. Again and again there are experiences of inner conflict, of oscillation between opposing worlds and contradictory inner tendencies.

The frightening question, 'Am I normal?', is widespread among adolescents. A teenager compares his or her sexual developments minutely to those of his or her peers, and each deviation of his or her own body is quietly hushed up. The search for sexual identity is fraught with many fears. While the child appears sexually neutral, the teenager lives for a certain time something like a male-female unity, an undecided hermaphroditism. Before the initiation of contra-sexual relationships many adolescents seek closeness to members of the same sex, partly from idealized devotion, partly from curiosity linked to the first sexual experiments. This is not homosexuality, but rather an expression of that wholeness which still joins masculine and feminine, undivided. In the course of further physical and sexual development, that other, the inner opposite, is increasingly lost, until it must be sought again in the other sex after maturity, and yet a new form of joining masculine and feminine can be experienced. But the path is long and, for many, painful and full of very frightening fears of being worthless and unloved, forever lost and abandoned.

Since the concrete possibility of a fulfilling love relationship is generally unrealistic, teenagers turn to the imagination. They write diaries, make up stories, join theater groups, immerse themselves in romantic novels. Masturbation, both to satisfy unfulfilled longings and as an experience of pleasurable tenderness toward their own bodies, often seems, even these days, to be burdened with fear of being found out or imaginary notions of being consumed from within.

Not only is the child at adolescence tossed hither and yon by his emotions, but so are his or her parents. The latter can feel that they are painfully abandoned too, can no longer communicate with their child, but experience him or her as a stranger. 'This isn't my child!' such parents say in desperation. But with this same consternation they express the extent to which they are themselves involved. Parents experience these far-reaching changes in their children as a call to their own mid-life transformations. Perhaps they even feel a twinge of jealousy. As children take their lives into their own hands, they are ever less suited to satisfy the needs and unrealized hopes of their parents. On the contrary, the adults are now challenged to attend, more than ever, to their own lives. This, too, is frightening, when they have been neglected all too long.

◇ ◇ ◇ ◇ ◇ ◇ ◇ ◇ ◇ ◇ ◇

Inner Experiences

Purberty occupies a central place in life, standing as it does at a crossroads: childhood is dying, adulthood is being born. It is a transitional process, and is thus comparable to birth and death. Such transitions are terrifying, narrow passes, where the individual must overcome a compression and intensification of his very existence, and which lead him far away from normal, everyday concerns. Above all, I receive hints from adolescents that they have inexpressible experiences of a transcendental nature, which they could never before, and may never again, feel with such intensity.

But compared with birth and death, puberty stands out in a particular, valuable way. Unlike newborns, adolescents have language which allows us to share in their lives, and, unlike the dying, they can return to us to tell about their experiences. This presupposes, however, that we understand their language and that we want to understand them. Unfortunately, our dealings with young people often founder on these assumptions. After all, at puberty the adolescent moves so far from everyday reality that even he doesn't understand himself any more, when he looks back on the darkest portion of his crisis of transformation. We need a special empathy and dedication to be able to fathom the development and experiences of a young person in this critical age.

The thoughts of adolescent boys and girls revolve around death and life: longing for death, wishing for life. Life and death become nearly synonymous, arbitrarily interchangeable. The border between them becomes permeable. On the one hand, teenagers are in great danger. They may kill themselves, sometimes intentionally, sometimes not. Some are swallowed up in unbounded experiences of the unconscious, approaching schizophrenia. But on the other hand, there is a readiness for deep experiences, which touch on the eternal and infinite. Such developments call to mind great feats of daring, like circumnavigation of the globe, voyages in space, or the descent of Herakles into the underworld, to Hades.

Who guides youth on their 'journey through the underworld' and, above all, guides them back again? Who stands beside them on this way inward? Who prepares them for their encounters with the shapes found in the depths of the unconscious—the archetypes of the collective unconscious, in the language of Jungian psychology?

However defiantly they behave, revolting against common authorities and calling into question traditional images of God, young people are basically looking for reliable authorities, basic rules, a meaning for their lives and rootedness in the Divine. Today's widespread 'enlightened' belief in the supreme power of reason alone, in the tools of modern thinking, leaves too little room for these deep needs. The archetypal expectations, which are deeply embedded in adolescents as primordial patterns, do not find an outlet, and must instead find, so to speak, emergency exits. Teenagers bolt into drugs or criminality, into often seemingly fanatical religious cults, or into gangs, where they are welded together by implacable laws. Some sink into loneliness, feeling understood by no one, held and supported by nothing, truly flirting with death. Yet others express their desperate search in physical or mental illness.

An intensive quest for the meaning of life underlies all these wrong turnings. I often understand adolescent depressive crises and states of panic as an outcry, as a call for help to make sense of their lives, a sense which they cannot find in their present environment. The question of meaning is a religious one, for how else does it happen that drug addicts, who flee from a feeling of emptiness and meaningless into intoxication, find firm ground for their withdrawal from drugs in religious communities?

Archetypal Patterns

The deeper process in puberty is characterized by ever-recurring, common patterns. Insight into this process was given to me in conversations with young people, by their dreams, fantasies, and daydreams, by their drawings and sandplay scenes. These are all communications from the mysterious depths of the unconscious, which may be expressed in the atmosphere of trust and protective shelter of psychotherapy.

Being alone is an important feature of the developmental path. Adolescents may sit of an evening, lost in thought, on a river-bank—if there is one—or build themselves little huts in the woods, to commune with nature and with themselves, with their inner nature. Sadly, many teenagers have no such romantic possibilities today, in our civilized world. For them, poor modern substitutes for solitude may be the Walkman, pinball, or computer games, in which they seem to hide themselves away, in order to find the aloneness they want. In psychotherapy, for example in therapeutic sandplay, we offer a protected place which supports their inner nature. One aspect of this solitude is regression into a safe and contained place, which allows energies to gather for the next step of the maturation process.

Closely related to the loneliness is the suffering of a symbolic *death*. At this time there is a need to do something radical to 'make an end', to shake off something that may have belonged to the familiar nest, be it parents, home, school, or whatever. The snake shedding its skin is a similar image. Parents often misunderstand their children in this step, and think they are ungrateful. Consequently, the child either shrinks back from further self-development in the face of all his guilt feelings toward the parents, or—in the better case—makes ever more drastic attempts to separate to get to his goal. Parents suffer from this; they must suffer. It feels to them as if their child is dying. Many adolescent emotional crises bear the marks of a symbolic death. This is particularly clear in the case of pubertal anorexia, where the afflicted girl takes flight into the spiritual at the expense of her earthly body. Yet this is equally an example of frustrated self-actualization or a form of needy self, which finds no other way through the deep conflict. These young women reach a state of utter dependency on their parents and environment, but at the same time their illness is a silent, and for that all the more vehement and fearful, revolt against the expectations placed upon them. They hang between the worlds.

Adolescents have a great desire for *ordeal*. Not only young men, but also young women want to prove to themselves that they can endure something. The ordeals must create fear, or else they do not have the important effect of conferring immunity. If teenagers find no appropriate opportunity for such ordeal, no outer framework, then here, too, they will hit upon a less-than-ideal solution, and undertake dangerous tests of courage or race wildly around hairpin curves on motorcycles. Some inflict cuts on themselves quite literally, in order to show explicitly the cut in their lives. It may mark the end of a life, rather than a new beginning. Young people do not want their feats to be overlooked. These are attempts to distinguish themselves clearly from their parents, not to be met with harmonious acceptance. Too-tolerant or chummy parents make a mistake in wanting to smooth everything over for their children. And in many places official political efforts to help youth also try too hard to 'make it easy' for youngsters, with superficial, material goods.

Death is not symbolic if it is not followed by a new *birth*. In their awkwardness and vulnerability, adolescents sometimes appear to be newborns. We are familiar with the shy teenage girls (in German 'Backfisch') who seem to communicate only in helpless giggles, or the teenage boys, ('Flegel') who are so bewildered by their sudden physical development that they seem hardly able to walk. Also, the insatiable demands of many young people remind us of the endless wants of a baby. This shows that they must learn a new way to relate to the world, after the earlier adaptation has been buried. Some announce their new beginning by getting new haircuts, repainting their rooms, or even giving themselves a new name.

With growing maturity there is a growing need for a *spiritual ordeal* and the related acceptance into a community. This also seems to me to be an expression of a new birth or rebirth. Such ordeals may take on a religious character, and may even be a search for revelation. Our Western forms of initiation ceremonies such as confirmation could have an important function in this sense. But if conventional institutions fail, sect-like groups have a powerful attraction for young people. Adolescents not infrequently take wrong turns. I have more than once had to admit them into the hospital as an emergency measure, when a psychotic crisis resulted from their turning to one or another foreign cult or to a new drug for 'help' in their search for salvation.

Rites and Rituals

In many cultures, especially among so-called primitives, impressive rites strengthen and support the transition from childhood to adulthood. Rites of passage, rites of initiation, also provide a protective shelter in this dangerous transition period. The young people are made aware in these ceremonies of the necessity of this step into life in dramatic, even frightening ways, but at the same time they are carried by them, contained within the collective order which goes beyond the familiar framework.

Ethnologists who have visited traditional cultures in foreign lands describe such initiation ceremonies in great detail. To a baffing degree, the individual stages of these rituals correspond to the patterns of experience appearing spontaneously among Western adolescents described above. In traditional cultures, the boys are set the task of leaving their weeping mothers behind and suffering a death in the isolation of the bush—only a symbolic death, but it must be experienced with dread and horror, like a true death. Thereafter the initiates are like newborns for a certain time, perhaps without speech and dependent upon passive nourishment, until, having endured all the physical and emotional trials, they are initiated into the secrets of the tribe by the village elders and may then be counted as adults.

These ceremonial occasions are reminders for the community, the participating members of village society, of the fundamental nature and laws of their culture or of all mankind, whose origin may have been forgotten. They are religious experiences (*religio*, from *religiare*, to re-link), reconnecting individuals and the community to their ancient origins and power. In this sense, our youth have the important mission of extending their own consciousness, for themselves, for their parents, and for society. Seldom do parents take up and make use of this challenge for themselves. And seldom is society prepared to question itself and, pressured by the young, venture a new consciousness. Here in Zurich we experienced this in a devastating way in the early 1980s. Youth unrest shook the structure of society to its foundations, and the local government was mobilized to prevent change in the formal social structure. It was not until several years later that a new consciousness began to dawn on a few individuals.

Does modern society offer the appropriate shelter and freedom to contain the transition from childhood to adulthood and make use of the energies that are released? The answer is clearly given by the great number of adolescents who come to us in crisis for psychiatric treatment or psychotherapy. Archetypal needs and expectations arising from deep within are not adequately met by society. These basic patterns become clear in the course of therapy, and they are lived out symbolically within the secure frame of the therapeutic relationship. The symbols serve as catalysts for the conversion of accumulated energies into a form which can be used for the further growth of the personality. Therapies often prove to be real initiation rites. While on an institutional level we still have a few ceremonies such as confirmation, these seem to me to be at best out-worn relics of rites of initiation, from which the effective symbol content has in large part been lost. And then all the greater is the search for substitutes, often in secret, hidden, underground.

Naturally, we cannot simply copy foreign cultures and cults. I look to them rather for an enriching validation, an amplification, of the innate patterns of transformation in puberty. Let us stay closer to home! And I do not address myself here only to specialists, therapists and anthropologists, but to the fathers and mothers of adolescents, whom I want to remind of the deep-indwelling, ordering principles of the soul of man. They offer themselves up to us in the apparent chaos of puberty. Can we not allow ourselves a bit more confidence in these powers as we observe and accompany our child through thick and thin as he faces the difficulties of adolescence?

I believe that the child too is relieved and encouraged to learn that he has not only been the recipient of help, patience, and care, but that it cuts both ways: he may also have had something to give to his parents. For this reason adolescents do not need perfect parents; quite the contrary. Nor do they need an over-friendly, ingratiating attitude as when, for example, parents want to be 'just one of the kids', instead of simply being themselves.

Adolescence seems to be not so much a distinct time of life as an ever-present pattern of transformation. While it certainly may have especially sweeping consequences during the period of physical and sexual maturation, it is in no way limited to that age. The transformation may falter halfway, and be resumed or completed in a later phase. In the course of a life, then, there are ever new 'puberty-steps', beckoning particularly when we are stirred and weakened by a physical or emotional crisis, as we were by the radical physical changes in younger years. The adolescence of our own children is especially suited to throw us back into our own adolescence, so that we can then make up what we previously missed.

The insights to be gained from the experiences of adolescents concern us all, whether we ourselves are stuck in puberty, or whether we are the parents or grandparents of teenagers, whether we, at an advanced age, further or again 'pubesce', or whether we find ourselves in a physical or emotional crisis, subject to the ancient patterns of death and transformation.

Two teenagers who are becoming adults are the heart of this book: 17-year-old Maria and 15-year-old Martin. It is obvious from their ages that neither was at the biological beginning of puberty. But while both were physically and sexually nearly mature, like many adolescents today the rest of their development had lagged a bit behind. The world of their feelings and their sense of their place in society were in the greatest turmoil. It is these aspects of the crisis which alert parents and educators, and for which they finally come to us seeking help and explanation.

I now invite you, my reader, to engross yourself in the stories of Maria and Martin, to allow yourself to be gripped and carried a bit outside yourself by them. I will not attempt to spare you from a feeling of helplessness, for it is an essential component of the experience of many adolescents—and their parents. But I will try to lead you to a new door into the inner world of children at puberty.

Maria

Background

It is no doubt a risky business for a man to wish to say something valid about a girl becoming a woman. I take it up, however, as a necessary challenge. Certainly a woman would paint a different picture of the girl and emerging woman from the one I present. But perhaps important complementary aspects can emerge precisely because they emerge out of reflections from a man's vantage point. I do not claim to offer a girl the power and authority of an old wise woman, but rather the love and devotion which is a brother's to give. When in my practice I ask a woman, in the course of or after a long therapy, 'What am I to you really? A father? A husband? A son?' I regularly receive the answer, 'Really a brother!'

The story of a young man should be compared to that of a young woman. Otherwise the observations and conclusions I draw about puberty would be incomplete, even questionable. But in a critical review of my therapeutic work with young women to date, I could not find an impressive case 'for show'. Why not? I had to recognize that the selection of 'my' patients is also an expression of my self.

Each therapy is a process, a becoming. As a therapist I don't stand outside events, and my work with Maria and her story is more than the others deeply tied up with my own development. She became a part of my education, teaching me about humanity as well as about therapy. When I reconsider my memories of it, I am astonished at my handling of the case, whose beginning now lies ten years back. One could say that I 'stumbled into' this treatment. For this reason, it would not be suited to a textbook on therapy. But the vividness of the events is in no way diminished by this. On the contrary, the feelings of the young woman for or against me (transference), and, the other way round, my feelings for or against her (countertransference) appeared with such intensity that they required that I consult with a more experienced person.

◇ ◇ ◇ ◇ ◇ ◇ ◇ ◇ ◇ ◇ ◇

Previous History

The family doctor referred Maria's father to me. He brought his wife to me and then he withdrew. His wife, while needing intensive therapy of her own, brought me in turn her problem-child, Maria. Out of discussions with these two came separate and simultaneous analytic work with each of them, mother and daughter, which has disadvantages, as we shall see. My position as double keeper of secrets was always trying. Over and over I wanted to give up the unusual arrangement. But it proved more powerful than I; I went on, as long as it was meant to be.

Today this double therapy is happily behind me, and with the secure vision of hindsight I can draw for myself some conclusions about the inner and outer lines of development of mother and daughter. Since the girl's attempts at self-development were closely bound up with the mother's problems, it seems to me all the better to place them both here, side by side. Maria's spirited obstinacy awoke her mother's own long-forgotten and neglected spirit, her very own life's work. And I came to sense that Maria, for her part, carried many burdens for her mother, who in turn had taken them over from her own parents. As vehemently as they outwardly turned away from each other, so all the more important were the things they had to say to one another. Despite my keeping of secrets on both sides, I became a conduit for secret, unspoken communications. When one was sitting with me, the other was also somehow present, and yet could, when needed, be shown the door. For me, both an invitation and a challenge! I would like to weave the occurrences in the mother's inner life into my reflections on Maria, and show their connection to Maria's development.

'Brother and Sister', the Grimm fairy tale, served as a main theme for me in my work with Maria. She herself drew my attention to this tale in the course of our 79 hours of therapy, since she was reminded of it by one of the 243 dreams which she told me during this time. I am presenting a short summary here:

20

Brother and Sister

*Little brother took his little sister by the hand and said,
"Since our mother died we have had no happiness . . ." Their
wicked stepmother beat them and let them go hungry. And so
they decided to go forth together into the wide world. The
brother was thirsty, but the stepmother had cast a spell on all
the springs along their way. The sister begged her brother not
to drink, for he would be turned into a tiger or a wolf. But at
the third spring his thirst was so great that she could no
longer restrain him. The brother took a drink and was turned
into a deer.*

*With the sister's golden garter tied around his neck, the
little animal lived peacefully with the girl in a tiny house in
the woods. But the deer soon heard the King's hunting horns,
and could not resist joining the chase. In the evening he
always came home again, saying, "My little sister, let me in!"
But then a hunter discovered his hiding place and his
password. The King learned of them, discovered the beautiful
sister and brought her to his castle as his wife. Little brother
lived happily as a deer in the palace garden. Soon the young
Queen bore a son.*

*The stepmother and her natural daughter learned of this
happiness and were full of jealousy. They crept into the palace
and suffocated the Queen in her bath with a fire of hellish
heat. The old woman laid her own one-eyed daughter in the
Queen's bed, dressed as the Queen. In the middle of the night
the true Queen cried, "How fares my child, how fares my
deer?" The King recognized her voice and was at first afraid,
but then sprang to her side and spoke to her. At that moment
she "came to life again, and by God's grace became fresh,
rosy and full of health." The witch was miserably burnt in the
fire, and her daughter was torn to pieces by the wild animals
in the forest. The deer was changed back into a man, and the
sister and brother lived happily together to the end of their days.*

Maria had long ago outgrown fairy tales. She expressed herself
as an adult, at least in writing. But in her dreams she stood as
close as a child to the world of fairy tales. It was as though she carried their knowledge deep within herself, and came into contact
every night with their age-old wisdom. In the end it was her

dreams, and not the therapy, which gave her inner security and support. The therapy served only to help her to relate to this inner world and to encourage her to stand up for it.

For months the 17-year-old girl had been causing mounting concern on the part of her parents and teachers. She was hopelessly depressed and failing in school; at home she would go off into a corner to sulk. She was the third of six children of a furniture-maker and bus-driver, and the eight family members shared a four-bedroom row-house apartment. Under pressure from the animated life of the other siblings and the parents, the apartment, as well as the mood of the family, threatened from time to time to "burst." Maria often jumped out of a window from the raised ground floor, or tried in some other way to "get some air".

The young woman approached her first hour with the psychiatrist not only with apprehension, but also with the secret hope that she would at last be helped. Now in tenth grade, she immediately began to talk about her problems in school, which she attributed to a concussion that she had suffered in the past year. But she had earlier had to repeat the third year of primary school, which she still felt to be an unbearable disgrace. Just then she was reading a book at home, *And There Was Light,* the story of a blind person who discovers an "inner light". What a beautiful overture to our joint psychological work! I presented Maria with a dream-diary, and already the following night she had a dream:

Dream
"I went shopping in the dairy store with a large basket. In the basket were two big, thick books, which were intended for Elsbeth. I bought only two little things. On the way home I could hardly go on, because my knee was shaking so badly that I almost fell down . . . My father laughed scornfully . . ."

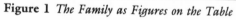

The Burden of the Family

Possibly the basket was so large, because she was supposed to buy a lot: the way I heard it, her parents had very high standards for her school and professional career. There she should 'buy' a great deal. But this load became heavy and difficult for her. She only wanted to buy something small. Her older brother Michael played piano very well, and was already beginning training as a teacher. Her older sister Elsbeth studied 'thick books' and played the violin; she would make something of herself. Then, after Maria, comes Christian, the parents' favorite son, who could do simply everything, especially playing the cello and painting. Felix was very sensitive and was often afraid of school, while little Verena put the others up to every possible prank and kept her parents on pins and needles.

Here we see the family constellation as Maria saw it: Christian, the favorite, stands between the parents (here portrayed as frogs). The two little ones, Felix and Verena (owls), stick close together.

Figure 1 *The Family as Figures on the Table*

Maria herself, as a cat, stands close to the two oldest siblings (brother as cat, sister as owl), with her back turned against her parents. Maria wrote an essay for me later about the family. The father's family stressed middle-class respectability and was very religious; "hypocritical", as Maria said. Everyone experienced the paternal grandmother as tyrannical. But when the father said, "Who knows how much longer we'll have her with us?" no one dared say what he thought to her face. The father had seven siblings, all of whom had accomplished something; only he himself was regarded as a failure and treated as an eternal child. He still courted recognition from his mother, in vain. His wife, Maria's mother, every so often called him "my seventh child." Even his children secretly whispered about his sketchy education. Only with difficulty and a lot of artistic improvisation could he feed his family and realize his ambitious educational goals for his children. In desperation, especially when he felt driven into a corner by his eldest, self-confident son and the "many women" in the family, he occasionally raised his hand, particularly to Maria. Recently his heart had been giving him trouble, and he had been making dangerous mistakes at work. It was for this reason that his family doctor sent him to me for psychological consultation. I found his spontaneous warmth agreeable, but it seemed also to distance him from himself. Instead of continuing to come, he sent his wife to me; she needed it much more than he.

The mother's relatives were much more interesting, said Maria. Maria's maternal grandfather, who came from Italy, was a shoemaker, and at night sang and played guitar in the bars. With the divorce of her parents Maria's mother was sent away to stepparents at an early age. They, like her natural parents, had died in the meantime, but she remembered them even now with horror. They discriminated against Maria's mother unscrupulously because of her Italian blood, called her "curbstone bastard" and the like, and sometimes brutally locked her in the cellar. Later, in her training as a hatmaker, she was humiliated again. She still had to arm herself against her mother-in-law, who could not get over the fact that her son didn't make a better match. No wonder that she would have liked her children to be seen as pure and unblemished. She identified with them, and for her, they served as a sort of bulwark again her wicked parents and step-parents, so that the whole family would appear beyond reproach.

To hear Maria talk one had to think, 'What an awful mother she had!' At the early age of 10 she no longer got a goodnight kiss like the others; then again, she didn't want one. But at the same time she secretly longed for mother-love, and took a whole army of stuffed animals to bed with her as a substitute. Maria was ashamed to notice that she had the same forceful, energetic way of walking as her mother. She had often thought about, or dreamed about, finding her 'real mother'. When one heard how Maria experienced her mother, a stepmother just like the one in the fairy tale stood before one's mind's eye. In the fairy tale, the wickedness of the stepmother provided the essential impulse for all that followed: 'Come, we will go forth together into the wide world', the children consoled each other, and then found their way. Maria carried this basic image (archetype) within herself, but there was also the concrete, outer mother. Nothing would have been more wrong than had I pointed an accusing finger at her. It would have served little purpose to the young woman on her way to her inner self. And as a doctor I would have soon lost the necessary confidence of the mother. It was, after all, she who had entrusted Maria to me for therapy. Maria, for her part, felt that what her mother had been threatening for so long had come true: that she would ultimately end up in a psychiatrist's care because something was wrong with her.

The Therapeutic Bond

While on the outside Maria did everything possible to keep her visits to me a secret, feeling them to be a shameful humiliation, she soon felt a strong bond to me. In her first dream we learn of her feelings of inferiority, especially toward her big sister, and of how hard it was for her to go on because of them. Sometimes she seemed paralysed. Many hours she sat across from me totally silent, and yet she seemed very eloquent in her silence. She thought of me as a powerful guide for her soul, and, when she assumed from the outset that I already knew what was wrong with her, she also overburdened me. I very much wanted to know how she saw herself in relation to me; assuming that she is a cat, what then am I? She holds her two hands wide apart: this big, "A King!" (Only many years later did she come to think that I was something like a big brother.)

I didn't feel like a king, but I left her her vision, which helped her for a long time. I vividly remember how she sat in her chair, mute and embarrassed with consternation, her cheeks red with shame or her tears hidden underneath her long hair, half yielding to the safe atmosphere of therapy, half defiantly turned away, wringing her ice-cold hands, bottling herself up, pounding her fist impatiently, aggressively on her knee. Sometimes I was moved afterwards to put my arm tenderly, consolingly across her shoulders. But she didn't allow me to do that; each time she shook her shoulders. Nevertheless, she told me later how important it was for her to feel my affection.

She was very grateful that what occurred in therapy remained a secret, even from her parents and teachers. She herself guarded the secrets zealously. When she sent me a letter between hours she implored me, "Don't say anything to my parents!" The fact that I was also involved in intensive work with her mother was a constant, if not insurmountable, strain. Sometimes she believed that I was in league with her mother. But however small and hopeless she seemed to me, she could nevertheless adopt something of the power and pride of a king in our private alliance, and take it with

26

her into her everyday life. I soon heard from both parents about the new boldness which Maria sometimes showed at home.

Her closely-guarded diary and dream book also provided a small, safe haven from all the family thunderstorms to which she otherwise felt so vulnerable. Her dreams became a living bridge to me, to her therapy, and through that to her true self, which only hesitantly and awkwardly revealed itself to the outside world. The dreams not only gave me deep insight into her heart; they served also to show me what went on around her in her concrete, daily life, what she thought and felt. Thus she could 'say' things to me, which under other circumstances she could never allow herself to speak out loud. The dreams also formed a bridge between conscious and unconscious, between outer adaptation and inner motives, between her everyday life and our therapy.

Night after night the dreams dealt with the seemingly hopeless school situation: the teacher hands back the notebooks, and hers is all marked with red; she comes late or doesn't go at all to school, taking delight in every excuse; she forgets the homework and tries to quickly copy it from others; she must repeat third grade yet again.

Once when the conversation was stalled for a long time, I suggested to her that we play a game together and met with a complete blockade. Here, too, she felt tested, on display, so deep ran her fear of teachers. And so I tried once to act out with her how things were going in school. Hesitantly, in a small voice she told me, "In school I only listen with half an ear, because I have so much else to think about . . ." "About what?" "About the fact that I'm simply incapable. But then I don't even really think about that, because I'm still half listening to the teacher."

The question of secrets was also subject matter for her dreams: she has secret notes which her father sees and snatches away, and he hits her because of their contents. They talk about changing coalitions with her siblings, who give her courage as examples and path-breakers, or from whom she indignantly turns away. Time after time one of her siblings has the function of substitute parent for her, now her big brother, now her big sister. She ventures to develop and strengthen her maturing ego under their care rather than that of her parents, who often experience her as overpowering and too demanding. Here, as well, the fairy tale 'Brother and Sister' is the *leitmotif* which guides her out of the bewitchment of the parental home.

✧ ✧ ✧ ✧ ✧ ✧ ✧ ✧ ✧ ✧ ✧

Captivity

Dream
"My whole family was in a strange place. We were captive,
together with others. We all sat in a large tent, but no one
kept watch. A few people escaped, but it was very difficult,
because we were surrounded by cliffs and barbed wire fences.
A few children tried to escape near the gate in the barbed
wire, but a guard stood there. Michael and I tried to climb
with a rope over dangerous holes under the snow and
crevasses in the glacier. I was afraid, so that we made almost
no progress. A man and woman passed us. Now came an
overhanging cliff. As we looked down from it, we saw a huge
sheet of ice which ran down at an angle. I thought we would
never get down, even though the people got through. I turned
back. When I came back to the tent, my parents, Elsbeth and
Christian were sitting in one corner, and Papa's sister was in
the other with her husband and two girls. The atmosphere was
very tense. They immediately told me that Grandma was
missing and wanted to commit suicide. My father sat there
completely silent and pale, while my mother was very
happy... I went back again to Michael, but he was already
on the big ice field and was building himself a tent out of
cloths. I went on again and looked for another solution."

While Maria peeked shyly out at me from behind her curtain
of hair, I studied this dramatic dream story, which seemed so out
of character for this timid child. But I soon learned to respect this
heroic daring, which first announced itself in dreams and only
much later could be translated into action in real life. The image
in the dream is of an inner reality, a seed of development possibilities to come. Seldom did a dialogue about the dreams ensue. I
had to be content with the dreams alone, associate to them and
amplify them myself. At most her facial expression told me
whether I had hit upon the right direction.

The dream tells of an imprisonment of the entire family. Maria's captivity involves them all. They live in a tent, and so are themselves in a place of departure and radical change. It seems to be the task of a few children to free themselves from this siege; this is, however, associated with many perils and fears. The ice shows how cold it is when one forsakes the family. The way leads down from the family's strange abode, to the ground. There is the risk of falling into treacherous abysses along the way. Fear itself hampers her progress. Her older brother leads the way. She goes part of the way with him, but then must find her own way. It seems to be a lonely path. She is not so far along as he, is still too closely tied to the family. When one looks at the dangerous and ice-cold stretch on the way ahead, it is indeed very understandable that she, despite all her rebellion and rejection, looks again to the family for support.

This inner situation accounts for her outwardly apparent state of being torn between closeness to, and distance from, her parents. The hinted-at suicide of her grandmother expresses partly Maria's own fantasies of suicide, and partly a leave-taking from the relatives who up till now had so imprisoned her.

As in Maria's dream, I want to come back to the family members again and again in the course of this book, and particularly to the mother, to see which path they must follow. I am very concerned with this look backwards because I so often see the consternation of parents who have been left behind by their adolescent children. Indeed, this book is addressed to such parents. On the one hand, the puberty and adolescence of their children could be a valuable, transformative chapter in the parents' own lives. And on the other hand, in the end only a renewal on the part of the parents allows the child to follow his very own path with a light heart.

Just as in the fairy tale of 'Brother and Sister', this journey across the huge ice field could serve as a *leitmotif* for Maria's future life path. It was a way along which she needed help; but this help was available within herself, for everything we dream, we have inside us. She frequently dreamt of the big brother who knew the way. She also dreamt often of me, as her soul-guide. Again and again he was somehow 'there, too'—as witness to events, often as someone who gave nourishment. Perhaps this symbolized some sort of 'provisioning' for the arduous journey; perhaps she saw my work as genuine caring, or wanted to see it as such. This guide, too, who knew the path ahead and gave nourishment, was available within her: it is, after all, her own dream. But this inner guide needed to be recognized and encouraged over and over again, for many dangers lay in wait along both sides of the lonely path.

Dream

"... I had to be at your office at eleven o'clock and took an eraser, a rope and the dentist's appointment card with me. I was hurrying because I had been worried the whole morning that I might be late... I was constantly thinking about what I could tell my schoolmates if they should ask where I was going. When the bell rang I sprang away quickly; a few girls were about to follow. But even though I summoned all my strength I could hardly get anywhere."

These were her associations to the three significant objects: I need the eraser to erase again what was said in the last hour; the rope can be used to tie together or to hang oneself (I amplify: perhaps to let oneself down when the path becomes rough, as in the dream above); she needs the appointment card to distract her friends from the fact that she goes to a psychiatrist. I understand the dentist to be also a symbol for a doctor of the psyche, who 'sinks his teeth into' a problem, gets to the 'root' of it, and hurts, too. She forgot her therapy hour more than once in her dreams. Again and again she awoke with a start after having dreamed that she nearly forgot the hour or was hopelessly late.

For a long time she again didn't say a word. I offered her a sand-tray, as it is used in therapy: perhaps this is more like her 'language'? While I read her dreams, our hands stroked together through the fine, moist sand in the sand-tray. I drew a sort of street in the sand, she continued it, then shyly, hesitantly reached for tanks and soldiers. After this hour Maria couldn't make up her mind to go home. She stayed by herself in the 'play-room' where, unobserved by me, she ventured to make another sand-picture. She destroyed it the moment I came in unexpectedly, but not without allowing me—as if by mistake—to get a quick glance at it. I saw an extremely neatly-built cemetery, with one grave set apart from the others. The next time, too, she didn't want to go home, and instead again played unobserved with the sand-tray. This time two scenes resulted which I was now allowed to photograph.

Sandplay as a means to psychological recovery was developed by Mrs. Dora Kalff. A choice of dry or moist fine sand is placed in a tray 49 by 72 cm, 7 cm deep. A large collection of miniatures from all spheres of nature, everyday life, and the fairy tale and mythical realms are available for the spontaneous creation of scenes. These may be pictures of the inner world or the secret world of the unconscious, or they may express the archetypal images of the collective unconscious, which in the course of a sandplay series accompany and support the process of self-development and becoming whole (individuation).

A sinister man who wants to murder Maria appeared in quite a few dreams, as well. Her mother had impressed such a picture of men upon her . . . Has she taken this evil-colored portrait of men into herself? Has it become a part of her, so unconsciously and autonomously effective that it threatens to become a hideous reality, as a suicide impulse? This image has, indeed, an objective meaning: her occasionally violent-tempered, punitive father. In many a dream he comes toward her with a pistol in his hand. When the wicked man has become 'part of her' (when the inner image of men which she carries within herself, her animus, has taken on such a negative, destructive quality), then the delicate, feminine side is threatened and must be protected. By a man? Therapy with me, a male therapist, here held dangers as well as opportunities. She could all too easily project the image of the evil, sinister man onto me. Her interminable, embarrassed si-

---

Figure 2 *Alone and in Danger (Sandplay)*

"I am standing on a high, naked hill, surrounded by a moat. From far away someone is shooting at me with a pistol. Behind me, below on the hill, sits a cat."

lence, which now and then seemed obstinate, aroused such suspicions in me, as did her great, paralysing fears, especially of male teachers, in school. Yet on the other hand there was the possibility that I could contribute something toward a positive image of her inner 'man', her animus, precisely because I am a man.

Her own sandplay scene suggested to Maria that she not look only to the outside for help, but rather that she rely on her own powers inside, on her own island. I too painfully felt the loneliness which this picture expressed. In the background, protected by the mountain from the man's gun, sits the cat, the animal of her choice, which symbolizes tenderness and defensive power. When she climbs down, protected by the shelter of the mountain, she can relate to the cat inside herself, her inner nature, as in the fairy tale 'Brother and Sister' where the deer and the young woman find their way.

Travels

Figure 3 *The Long Way in the Wind*

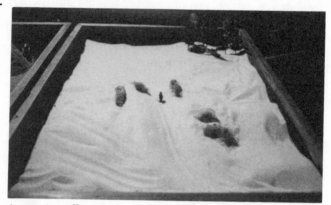

A man is walking on a long, desolate path. Only in the corner, in the woods, is there a solitary house. This scene is the memory of a picture in which the wind was blowing hard, said Maria.

In this second sand-tray from the same day something has begun to move, in contrast to the stiff, aggressive restraint of the first sand-play. Maria has gotten herself going. She has enough courage to go her own way, even if it is long and lonely. The green trees in a small corner point hopefully toward growth. There is also a place to live there. I learned from her parents that she seemed to feel better now at home—was beginning to furnish her corner cozily. Although it is true that she got along very well with her big brother Michael, especially because he would bravely stand up to their parents, she could not discuss her most personal problems even with him. There remained only the solitary path.

Another important inner figure who kept vividly coming up in Maria's dreams was the child. It took on many forms. It grew younger and younger in age; at the beginning there were schoolchildren, later small children, then infants. These were children in need, wounded, handicapped, discriminated against, mute and speechless children who peopled Maria's dreams. They seemed grateful when the dreamer adopted them to herself. "That would also be a profession for me," she remarked in her dream journal, since at that time the search for a possible occupation was becoming increasingly urgent. The neglected child in her was crying out for help and care—and receiving it, from Maria herself. The therapist in her was becoming active and devoting itself to all the neglected, maltreated parts of her, so that they would once again grow strong.

One day, when Maria seemed quite cheerful to me, I gave her watercolors, paper and pencil. I was astonished at the dismal picture which came about:

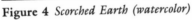

Figure 4 *Scorched Earth (watercolor)*

Burning houses, a huge black cliff, and in between a small, black man. Maria says that she must get over the cliff, but she cannot. She just doesn't have the courage to attempt it.

While Maria was painting, I read her dreams, which were often so numerous and extensive that I could only give brief attention to many of them.

Dream
"We all knew that my mother would die the next day . . . I ran
into the woods and cried. Then I came into a house, where
Elsbeth and you were. You had your clinic there . . ."

In a few other dreams the death of a man occurred with slight
variations, the man occasionally taking the form of her brother
Michael. What had happened? Or better, what inner occurence
was in the wind? Objectively, nothing spoke of an imminent
death of either mother or brother. The painting of the great fire
suggested to me that it is less the concrete mother who dies, but
rather that sense of domestic-motherliness, the intimate world,
the familiar nest of childhood, for which the mother is a symbol.
The big brother, her cohort in revolt against their parents, is going
his own way.

The painting of 'The Scorched Earth' shows Maria lost between the destroyed home and a forbidding wall of rock, in which
the face of a furious monster seems hidden, a harbinger of an om-
inously unknown, seemingly insurmountable, future. The tiny
man hangs in limbo; there is no turning back, he can only go forward, but he lacks the courage for that. I, with Maria, experienced
this feeling of being lost for a bit. The dream of the woods helped
us along: in the woods she finds the peace to give way to her feelings and cry herself out. In the woods, too, she finds help: her doctor together with her big sister, to whom she increasingly looks for
closeness, 'woman to woman', even at home. Following the dream
I suggested to Maria that she paint what there is to see behind the
mountain. From this came the painting of the 'Sunset/Sunrise'.

The freedom and distance in this painting did us both good,
after the hopelessness of the previous picture. I asked her,
"What's missing in this picture?" Maria replied, "Men, animals,
plants," whereupon she enlarged the green bushes. Whether it is
sunrise or sunset is not specified, so that this sun maintains a
timeless, even eternal character. It remains indefinite whether the
continued ship voyage over the great water leads to new horizons,
or down to the unfathomable sea bed. Subsequent dreams helped
us to foresee the journey to come.

A long series of dreams dealt with water, in its most varied
manifestations:

Dreams of Water
"Two large ships were sunk in a storm, and thousands of men
are lying drowned in the water. I thought immediately of

Figure 5 *Sunset/Sunrise (watercolor)*

Michael... Then came the others with the news that Michael was on another ship. I was glad..."

"I was on a big ship. I was always looking down at the water, to see where it was the deepest. It looked very frightening..."

"It was gloomy out, and raining. When I came home I went into the cellar and wanted to turn the main water faucet on, because I didn't want to go on living..."

"The whole class was at a lake... Afterwards I sat off to the side on the bank. The sky was grey and cloudy, and the lake was dark, like before a thunderstorm. Suddenly waves came, which drove me out into the lake. I pulled myself together and tried to reach firm ground again. I ran away, but then after a long time looked back at the lake, and thought about how it would be if I were to jump in."

"I was walking to B's house. Suddenly Christian came too. He went a different way than I did. I looked where his way went. The path was under the ground. Water was flowing out of a pit. I said that it was dangerous, because one didn't know when more water would come. Finally I arrived at the house, out of breath because I had hurried. You were also there..."

"... A snowy landscape... Felix was playing... He fell

*through the ice, but he could swim. My mother was just about
to scream for fear. I said that she should keep quiet at once,
or else Felix would be frightened and wouldn't be able to
swim any more . . ."*

*"It was raining hard. The sky was grey and gloomy. The
rivers and streams were flooded from so much rain. I waded
through a stream and almost didn't find the way home again.
I found A's body on the ground . . ."*

*"I was running with Michael and Christian—suddenly we
were riding in the train, going between a river and a lake.
The water had risen incredibly high, so that I was always
frightened we would drive into the lake. The water reached
about halfway up the side of the train, but didn't touch it."*

The reader may well feel nearly flooded by all the water after
reading these dreams. It was that way for me. How must Maria
have felt, when night after night she had to do battle with this
water! Perhaps the reader will get a small taste of it here. Why
does water play so central a role for this young woman? Why was
she built so close to the water, for which her tears, her bedwetting
(or her memory of it), and her damp ("weeping") hands are also
outer expressions? What does the water in the dreams stand for, if
one translates it into the young woman's real life? Outside the
context of Maria's dreams, we can learn something about the
meaning of water in general. It is:

—a supporting element, but in whose waves one can also go
under, lose the bottom, depending on the mood of the water or
the quality of the boat;

—an attractive element, in whose 'arms' one can from time to
time want to be engulfed, or in which one can want to simply 'let
onself go under';

—an expression of feelings such as grief, sadness, shame, dis-
gust, zest for life (dark clouds, grey rain, tears, bedwetting, filthy
mud, pleasure in swimming). Repository for the most private secrets and refuge of personal security;

—portrait of the life path: river travel, sea journey;

—symbol for life in general: the current of life, the sap or juice
of life, to be 'full of juice', especially at the age of puberty—
menstruation and other 'juices';

—the dark and unknown, partly dreaded, partly longed-for.
The wish to get to the bottom of things, the fear of being
inundated;

—the symbol of a ship: the spiritual principle, which makes the journey through the waters of the unconscious possible. Similar to the ship of the church;

—biblically, the Flood, Noah's Ark;

—symbolism of Christianity: purifying and transforming power of water, the water of life and death, baptism.

Maria had many essential experiences through the varied contacts with water in her dreams; she 'steeped' herself intensively in basic principles of life. She got a sense of the invisible powers, the secret, unknown motives, which guide outer events as if with an invisible hand. Great respect for this inner world increases, the more one attends to it and takes it seriously. The water itself symbolises this obscure world of the deep soul. And the qualities which the water in Maria's dreams takes on make us both afraid and awed. To remember dreams, write them down, and then think about them means to bring light into the unconscious, to become more familiar with things which are unfamiliar and foreign-seeming, but which are nonetheless deeply our own. Maria's constant and faithful accounts of her dreams were an indication to me that this world had something to say to her. Still today, ten years later, she feels supported and guided by a power which she experienced at that time through her dream work.

Dreams are more than simply reactions to, and commentaries on, the events of the day; they are also more than simply 'weather reports' for things in the immediate future. The unconscious recognizes a completely different way of dealing with the boundaries of space and time than we have learned from our upbringing and everyday experience.

Maria's water dreams indicated paths which I will pursue in what follows, for they touched upon some difficult questions which are of consuming concern for Maria's parents, as well as for other parents of adolescents.

The Death of Childhood

The wish to die kept coming up urgently, as when, for example, Maria wanted to just let herself go in the waves. The concern that a young person's death fantasy might one day become a reality, even if only by accident, is unfortunately justified. When young women drop threatening hints, they seem to clearly intend that the parents worry. In this way they are looking for a special kind of caring, now that they have painfully learned that they are no longer the sweet, innocent child, admired from all sides.

But over and above that, mainly only tacitly, they are indicating something else: a death creates distance from childhood and from the parents. And only with the creation of distance can the new life of the young adult begin. This is why parents' worry about their children seems to me to be so justifiable and important. Children must be able to deeply experience that their parents have externally as well as internally distanced themselves from 'their child', who is no longer theirs, and no longer a child. For this reason parents' attitude must not express the wish to hold on to the happy state of childhood, but must instead be mournful, attentively accompanying and confirming the painful course of events. This demands a great deal of parents who believed that they owned their child.

As the therapist for both mother and child I could experience these events at close hand and from both sides. Maria was regarded by her mother as her biggest problem child, with whom she was deeply connected in sorrow and in fury. Maria was also the most similar to the mother; both her thoughts and her behavior reminded the mother of her own youth—but this had been so oppressing and wretched that she would really rather have completely forgotten it. She still had to battle with the feeling of worthlessness she had experienced so hopelessly at that time, which had been given to her by her parents and step-parents, and then later also by her mother-in-law. The memories of her own youth may have been one reason for her enormous rage against this child, who evoked them. As her companion and listener I became an indispensible repository for her tears and hurts.

In one of the mother's dreams her attitude toward the growing, maturing and separating children was clearly visible:

A Dream of Maria's Mother
"I was picking raspberries; the berries were falling down to the
ground, laughing and getting dirty. Then I turned to some
other berries, to pick them. Behind me new berries kept
ripening; again and again I looked back angrily."

She had many helpful ideas about this dream. At home she was a very efficient, clean housewife. Keeping house demanded great energy of her, with so many hungry and dependent children—seven, if she included her husband. The children made fun of the way she busily kept house. She was amazed at the way her smaller children were maturing faster than the older ones: "What a pity!" The plants in her garden served as a substitute for babies. She often had the fantasy that the berries had faces or were living things. She always felt that she must especially hurry while picking berries. Then she became very involved in describing to me the individual children and how much they were already going their own ways. While there was a trace of praise to be noticed here, most of all there was genuine anger.

With Maria we enlarged upon her reflections a bit. It was with joy that she noticed, nearly 18 years before, that she was expecting her third child. She carried each child, Maria included, very close to her, with care and deep love. But that time she was recurringly troubled by emotional ill-feelings. Her mother (the natural one) had given her money and an address so that she could "get rid" of the child. "Should I, as wife and mother, also be a murderess? No." Maria's fetal movements were quite strong early on, especially when the mother wanted to lie down to rest. Today she was still full of emotion as she described the newborn little Maria to me. "A miracle! The sweetest little baby there ever was." She and her husband were astonished at how active Maria was at an early age: in no time she kicked herself out of her diaper or lay crosswise in the bed.

Playing, running, talking (especially "No" and "Me")—she learned everything early. She was 'quicksilver' or 'a powderkeg'. Elsbeth turned into a sort of "little mother" for the boisterous Maria. Maria was jealous of Christian, who worried their parents as a baby, when he was born and for a long time afterwards. She strictly refused to sit on the potty, and made herself so stiff that one could lay her across it like a board. She still wore a diaper her first year of kindergarten. Until third grade her bed was wet almost every night. She became the entertainer for her siblings, and placed herself on the kitchen table and put on plays. Her laughter was positively infectious to the others. In kindergarten she was happy and very attentive. In school, however, she had a lot of trouble. And worries about school weighed increasingly on her parents, who felt nearly consumed by them.

And this daughter now falls laughing into the mud like, so to speak, a ripe little fruit, before the eyes of her mother, who stands there helplessly! Maria was enormously impudent at the moment and laughed scornfully if her parents worried about her gloomy job prospects. The father obviously needed the children to fulfill his fatherly pride: they should show by their careers that he has achieved something, at least through his children. The more Maria's parents urged her, the more she opposed their expectations. Instead of a nurse, as her parents wish, she was thinking of becoming a bell-ringer in a small village in the Tessin (the southernmost region of Switzerland).

The following three dreams give a glimpse into Maria's brave search for her own path. Between the second and the third lies only one day, on which, incidentally, she had a first affectionate rendezvous with a neighborhood boy.

Three Dreams

"I tried several times to go over the bridge, but the fear that it could collapse was too great. The sun didn't come any more, and everything was gloomy and oppressive."

"We found ourselves in a strange place. There was a high bridge over which I had to go in order to get any further. But I had such a fear of stepping onto the bridge that I refused to go on, despite the fact that Elsbeth called to me again and again that I should just run. Then Michael ran across the bridge to show that it held. Nevertheless, I didn't have the courage, and I started to cry. Suddenly an unfamiliar girl came and stepped across the bridge. Finally I dared to do it, too."

"We came again to the bridge, as in the last dream. This time, though, Michael, Christian and I were riding bicycles. Despite the fact that I was a little afraid, I rode over.

Somewhere in the middle Christian slowed down and wanted
to stop. I just went on, so that he was forced to go on or I
would have run into him. I thought that once we were moving
he should keep riding, too." (The previous evening: the first
meeting with a boyfriend!)

These three dreams indicate the essential breakthrough: Maria is leaving the safe world of childhood, without succumbing to the temptation to let herself be engulfed in the waters of the unconscious. A bridge has been built that she can rely on.

Maria began at that time to meet the neighborhood young people behind her house in the evening. We recognize what a great, perhaps much longed-for lift that gave her, when in her dream she rides boldly over the sinister, previously dreaded bridge, even as the driving force. She also dreamed that she was picking some ripe cherries which tasted wonderful, but then later became uncertain that they were not forbidden. Her cheeks were glowing red as she told this dream. This development, too, her parents observed with open suspicion, stamped onto them by a puritannical upbringing. Maria dreamed once of her parents at that time: they had gotten onto the wrong train. To me it was clear that she was going rapidly, emphatically her own way. At this time I spontaneously began to address Maria with 'Sie' (the formal 'you', reserved for adults, as opposed to the familiar 'du' used with children), although she then forbade me to use it afterwards.

At seventeen Maria was not early- but rather late-maturing. It had been made more difficult for her to leave childhood, whether because of her unfullfilled longing for love, or whether because her parents loved her in their own way too much and did not want to let her go. Yet her remaining a child was inconsistent with the inner plan, which now wanted to be realized in other, alternative ways.

Emergency Solutions

The inner plan of development, the basic human pattern according to which children change into adults, is recognizable in this girl's pictures and dreams. Could this pattern be lived out in her real life? Up to this point a few things were in the way, so that she had to try emergency solutions. Paths sketched out symbolically are converted step by step into concrete acts, when the outer world opposes their being realized in any other way. A familiar example is of young people, who, to compensate for their inferiority feelings, admire a flying Superman in the film and then fatally convert this symbol into concrete action. A true, completed suicide may seem to be the only remaining resolution for adolescents in a desperate situation. But much more common are suicide attempts. These have the important function of shaking us up and marking a break, so that the prelude to a new beginning can develop. For this reason alone suicide attempts are to be taken very seriously, even if they appear "demonstrative, hysterical, and pleading" or are (unfortunately) trivialized in some other way. It is extremely important that these acts of desperate bravery are not overlooked, for otherwise they were made in vain and must be repeated, possibly with a fatal outcome the next time.

It is no wonder that Maria was depressed because of her failure at school and her feeling of not being understood at home and that she flirted with death in her fantasies and dreams. It was nearly always a death in water, which sounds additionally like a wish for protection through immersion in the realm of the unconscious.

It is exactly this quality which is also sought in drugs: flight from consciousness and the harsh examination of reality. This emergency solution, too, was hinted at in a few of Maria's dreams: "Give me a shot!" In reality she did use hashish and pain killers. There was unfortunately a drug circle around the youth center she often visited. Maria fell under its spell and her older brother wrote me an alarming letter. Then once, in a confused and despondent mood, she took an especially large dose of pain pills, partly out of dependency and partly intending suicide. The resulting emergency stay in a clinic was an important, awakening turning point. For a while she was free of all parental expectations, free for once to follow her own inner direction.

From the beginning Maria was also open to an emergency solution of an entirely different sort. She had a schoolmate, Ramona, who had had to be admitted to a psychiatric clinic due to a psychotic (schizophrenia-like) crisis. Because of this Maria had a special interest in the girl. Maria went often to the clinic to visit her, and many dreams bring her up.

In these dreams Ramona went "on a great trip", appeared "gypsylike", wore a peculiar dress, and spoke in a wild, contradictory rush. Her voice was curiously unnatural and she was cross-eyed. One time she wore odd black glasses and had expressionless eyes. It was as if she were from another world. Ramona mostly had drawings in her school notebook (so it said in a different dream): many faces, with one half sunken and haggard and the other normal, and landscapes that were the same way, with shadowy and sunny sides. She appeared again and again in the dreams, to Maria's surprise and great joy, and she was always somehow surrounded by a strange, mysterious aura. Once Ramona suddenly disappeared, leaving behind a book which at first Maria wanted to show me, but then did not dare to. Maria followed the course of Ramona's going insane and then becoming well again with devoted attention. She tried faithfully to keep the distant, moon-like world which Ramona inhabited connected to ours with her visits and letters. In Maria's dreams Ramona even came once to my office, and once to my vacation resort, where she said, "Here the complexes go away."

Maria experienced a deep affinity with the sick girl. Something in Maria was just as ill, and found a counterpart in the other. She could experience herself in the other girl, without having to consciously admit to herself and others, "I, too, am just as sick." In Maria's circle, especially among her schoolmates, it was considered highly suspicious when someone had anything to do with such "psycho-things", which is why she kept her visits to me a closely-guarded secret. On the dream level she devoted herself to her sick friend, giving care, encouragement, and comfort, and in the process she secretly cared for, encouraged, and comforted her own mad, split-off side. On the other hand, this inner spirit figure was also a guide for Maria. The dream ego let herself be taken by the hand on a healing journey through the illness, on "a great trip" where "the complexes can be lost". Ramona is a personification of the night and shadow side of life, the dark, mysterious powers which Maria felt so strongly in herself, but which had so little place in the outer world of her daily, life, particularly at a time when school and the choice of profession were making many concrete demands of her. Even Ramona herself suggested an inclusive wholeness, a union of the opposites, in her pictures of the double aspect of faces and of the landscape ('light and shadow sides').

The Animal Within

In the fairy tale 'Brother and Sister', Maria was at the third spring, where her thirsty brother was turned into an animal by the bewitched water. It is indeed a kind of madness when the animal-like part of oneself, the natural instinctual part, suddenly takes on bodily form. Maria remembered that her parents had once said that she must be possessed. This time of change and transition implies an encounter with one's own instinctual nature. But there is also the danger of separation, of the dissociation of the two sides. Just as the golden garter holds the two sides together in the fairy tale, so Maria was at pains to maintain the contact with her crazy (dissociated) friend.

The physical changes in puberty, the strange feelings which rock a pubescent girl, must seem very, very foreign. 'I feel like I'm bewitched', girls of this age have said to me before. Some, like Ramona, break up completely, and then are also called bewitched, dissociated or schizophrenic by outsiders. The 'normal' ones react partly with fear and partly with respect.

In the helping professions, one tends to want to pull these split-off creatures back to grounded reality. But I doubt that we would do justice to the secret concerns of these 'patients'. With Ramona, Maria showed that she was aiming toward wholeness, that is to say, pointing out to us also the reverse side of the coin, the hidden shadow side. Maria also showed us a way to deal with the 'sick' side: it is necessary to accept its message and bring it over to us, to link it with the normal world, to integrate the dissociated parts. It seems to me that a one-sided defense against the crazy portions only reinforces the fascination and attraction of that side, and so leads to a strengthened dissociation, splitting the opposites further apart instead of bringing them closer together.

It was Christmas again. Maria silently slipped me a small basket of sweets she had made, with a hand-drawn card, on the back of which were the words, "Thanks for everything!"

How 'communicative' this quiet young woman was in her pictures! It also looked this way inside her: half dilapidated, over-

Figure 6 *The Bewitched House (drawing)*

grown with weeds and flowers, almost like the castle of Sleeping Beauty. Amazing, that a jug is still standing above, in the window! She drew the picture with quite a bit of love and devotion, and what she had to say seemed to be of great concern to her. Here are a few attempts at translation for us adults who are so very limited to the language of words:

—I can't live in my house any more.

—That would be a place for me, because that is exactly how it looks inside me!

—Here, in this lonely place, I would like to live completely alone, just me, so that I can finally find myself!

—I'd like to get down to it here for once and rebuild the whole house from the ground up; will you help me?

—Or is it a witch's house?

The fairy tale 'Brother and Sister' offers its own helpful instructions for the healing of bewitchment. Love and hate are equal forces for the removal of an evil curse. Love: the king falls in love with the young girl, brought about by the bewitched animal, whose tracks lead to the lonely little house in the woods. The love between Brother and Sister holds the opposites (man and animal) together, so that they do not lose each other during the bewitched separation; the golden garter serves as a golden bridge. Hate: the evil stepmother and her ugly daughter follow the dictates of their jealousy and kill the young queen. Then again love, which conquers all: the king is courageous enough to respond to the voice of his wife from the hereafter, by which she again becomes flesh and blood. All this is the prerequisite for the last stage of deliverance: the witch is burned, the false queen is thrown to the wild animals, and the deer again becomes the little Brother.

Applied to Maria's living, concrete situation this means that the contact with the inner animal must be maintained. The connection is as valuable as gold, like the golden garter, because it makes sure that this important part remains, and does not go its own way and become autonomous, that the 'animal' does not break through and out, as it can be experienced in the complete dissociation of a psychic illness.

Dream
"We had school on a large ship that goes around the Lake of
Zurich. On the ship were many animals, camels and great
strange birds, built in a complicated way... My father said
that if a storm came, the ship could go down. Suddenly the
ship turned 180 degrees. Everything fell out. I was worried
about the animals."

We paid great attention to the animals which accompanied Maria in her dreams. Often they appeared suddenly and unexpectedly, as though they came from another world with which they are trying to bring us into contact. We can look upon these animals as some of the girl's natural and instinctive powers, which attract her attention for the first time when they are neglected in the outer life situation. They then have a compensating, balancing effect.

As an example, I will set out one of the encounters with the animal within more precisely. The starting point was a:

Dream

*"Astrid U. was running around with crutches and a broken
leg. I asked her what happened. She avoided answering. Then
I asked Gertrude. After some hesitation she said that Astrid
wanted to help someone out of prison, and it had happened
then. We went with Astrid to the hospital. On the way we
encountered a mountain goat. I was afraid of it. It started to
come at us with its horns. I sprang quickly away from there,
with the thought that it might be rabid, too."*

She told me this dream as we were walking through the woods.
Handicaps and injuries were in many of her dreams, probably as
an expression of the idea that she could not make full use of her
possibilities. Many of those hurt or handicapped dream figures
were small children, so we paid special attention to that stage of
her life. In this dream the handicap is threefold: one person is in
prison, the liberator has a broken leg, and on the way to the hospital a dangerous mountain goat stands in the path. It is most urgent to overpower the goat, so that the healing of the broken leg
and the liberation from prison can happen. In order to get better
acquainted with the nature of this animal, I proposed to Maria
that she make a drawing of it:

Figure 7 *The Stubborn Mountain Goat (drawing)*

Maria drew 'her' animal so sensitively that the mountain goat appears almost alive here. We came around to speaking about her own goat-like nature. Did she not also place herself obstinately in the way? For example, when she stayed so stubbornly silent? Such a goat can also express aggression and anger. The dreamer's fear with regard to rabies appears exaggerated, though. She is just not close enough to her animal. Too, Maria had learned at home that children should be clean and obliging. There, the children who acted like good little lambs were preferred. There was no place for such a mountain goat buck, and so he had begun an all the more destructive independent existence, expressed in the form of self-doubt and suicidal impulses. He held back her progress and placed himself right across her life's path, as is clearly shown in the drawing: the way leads from lower left to upper right, known to psychologists as a positive direction out into active, conscious living. The path leads out of the woods, becoming clearer, but overhead it looks gloomy and threatening. One tree has already been torn apart by a storm or thunderstorm.

The mother, too, encountered various animals in her dreams.

A Dream of Maria's Mother
I was sitting on the bench in front of the house. An animal
came closer to me there. I was astonished and horrified at
what it could be. Certainly an animal, but what kind of
animal? Black, smooth skin, floppy ears, nearly human face,
ungainly body, sturdy legs, ape-like paws. The strange
creature sat down right next to me. He looked peacefully
around. I immediately felt a good contact with him, coming
from within. I stroked him on the head and told him that I
feel that people never understand me.

I felt this encounter with the dream animal to be a true coming into her own. She needed to discover and appreciate qualities which she would much rather get rid of in herself, but which she lovingly accepted in this animal: the "black skin", for example, leads us to think of her Italian ancestors, contempt for whom was drilled into her as a child. The "stocky legs" also belong to her, since she looked "firmly rooted to the ground". The kind animal helped her to come to like this quality, too. The "ape-like" paws were a reference to her creative inclinations, which she soon put into action: out of simple attempts with clay she gradually developed a complete potter's studio. I was impressed by the peaceful, loving tone which she adopted toward her animal nature.

Another dream animal was a small donkey who asked her to be his mother. And once she dreamed of a giant bear, which brought the discussion around to her excessive, 'smothering' motherliness.

Animals were in many respects important teachers for this woman. She always found it difficult to use her natural energies appropriately. On the one hand she disregarded both her own and her children's natural, human limitations; again and again she demanded achievement, was hunted and haunted by duty: 'I will, I must!' On the other hand, she rejected certain other natural sides, which had to do with sensual desire, in herself as in her children. From the beginning she had considered sexuality 'disgusting'. Outbursts of anger and the like were also frowned upon. She was at pains to ensure that her children (and she herself) appeared, at least to the outside, like angels.

The Shadow

The idea that anger and aggression are permissible human emotions seemed to be entirely new to Maria. Later, to test me, she would give me a faint blow, or briefly point a toy crossbow at me, after which she always became afraid and wrote me an embarrassed letter of apology. She had to discover that she could have real feelings of anger against me, her very much admired doctor, and she worried that she could lose me if these were to appear. Maria had learned in the meantime to show aggressive feelings at home, too, to the indignation of her parents, to whom I tried to explain such feelings as an important success of the therapy. In school she performed in the drama class production: 'Now They are Singing Again: An Attempt at a Requiem' (Max Frisch). At the premiere her mother was also in the auditorium. Her presence nourished Maria's 'rage, power, and courage'. The role in the play enabled her for once to show these emotions to her mother and to all the world. To me it was clear that Maria brought one of her 'animals' to life in this way.

With this we are again back to the mother, who plays a decisive role, in both the fairy tale and in reality.

The mother followed the latest development with sneaking anxiety: Maria fell in love with a neighbor boy. It was only a little skirmish, but alarming enough for the mother. It also didn't escape her that Maria was settling down in the therapy with me, was feeling secure and accepted. I now saw the fact that both mother and daughter had me as a therapist to be technically a real mistake. Keeping the same loyalty to both, and keeping the secrets of each from the other, became an exhausting challenge for me. Therefore I suggested to the mother that she interrupt her therapy for a certain time for the sake of her daughter, who needed it more. I did not foresee that I had thus brought about the conditions of the fairy tale: Maria triumphed as the chosen bride of the King, while the mother's feelings were understandably hurt. I was finally compelled, then, to continue the former double therapy.

Today I see the advantage of this arrangement. Like many

other things which just turn out well without great planning, in retrospect it proved to be the right arrangement. It is as if a secret plan which dwells within things and man comes to fruition 'by accident' rather than through rational planning. For Maria and her mother it was correct that I go on working with both of them. At least two participants belong to the process of separation, which was for both a central part of the work. And this arrangement was particularly convenient for considering all the events together, especially from the larger perspective of the fairy tale.

What advice do the events in the fairy tale have to give to the mother? It must first be said that Maria's mother is neither a stepmother nor evil. But it was the stepmotherly and evil aspects which Maria had to tackle, partly objective characteristics of the real mother, partly entirely subjective, projected, ways in which Maria experienced her. It seems to me that it is very important to see the individuality of the parents, too, their own personal development, which is in turn embedded in a sequence of generations and determined by it. The finger eternally pointed at 'the evil parents' by child psychologists who love the children all too much has already made many parents uncertain and ruined many therapeutic efforts.

In the family drama of the fairy tale 'Brother and Sister' we could just as well put Maria's mother in the place of the princess, and then three suitable castings may be considered for the evil stepmother: her mother, stepmother and mother-in-law. Incidentally, the play of powers in a fairy tale is not tailored exclusively to a certain family, but instead is about universally valid (archetypal) patterns, which have significance everywhere and in all times.

We therefore do not want to cast Maria's mother only in the evil role of stepmother and witch, but rather let her become also the King's bride. She, too, was looking for herself. It was a long search, for which until now she had hardly found the courage, given the crushing conditions of her background. The upsurge of life Maria was now experiencing irritated her enormously, for she must have recognized that the freedoms which Maria was now taking would never be hers. This stirred up rage against her own parents. And at the same time she felt very restless. Nevertheless, it was not too late for her to set off on the path of her own life. She felt ignominiously left behind by her children, with whom she had so lovingly and powerfully bonded. She suffered unspeakable pain on that account. In rage against her growing brood she once cried out that never again would she want to give birth should she come back into the world. But finally she had to admit that her children, most especially Maria, were in many areas able to show her the way.

She did not fundamentally change all this, but now and then she would show a thoughtfulness, and gradually things began to move and she could give up many ingrained patterns. She had found new ways of being together with her husband. They ambitiously freed themselves from their duties and spent a long weekend in the Tessin, from which they returned warmly united, as if from their honeymoon.

For her part, Maria appeared thoroughly inspired by her affair with the neighborhood youth, and grateful that I diverted her mother's attention from the affair toward her own life. She felt physical desire in her own body when she gave herself up to certain pleasurable discoveries in the shower. Yet the newest experiences meant far more to her as well, and brought her to new shores, as did the dream in the night following the first little love adventure, where she was the driving force behind the passage over the bridge. I believe these were the key experiences of her adolescence.

To tie up the central thread of the fairy tale in this respect, as well: Each, daughter as well as mother, found her 'royal consort'. And in the therapy, which they both continued with me, each could feel herself to be the intended. Maria had indeed ceremonially acknowledged me 'King', and the mother in her way inundated me with so much positive transference that I could feel myself to be at least a king. It is also a great moment for the therapist when something like a 'royal wedding' can be celebrated. It is a symbolic wedding, which seals a union of the inner opposites. Woe betide the therapist who is tempted to convert this symbolic act into an outer action and see himself as the concrete lover of his patient. He would lose the magical power which is so important for healing.

The New Child

It is the natural course of things, just as the fairy tale would have it, that the King's bride has a child. I would like to here give only a small selection of the countless dreams about this inner event:

A Dream of Maria
"I had a small child. It lay suddenly before me on my homework desk . . . I was delighted about the little one. It had blue eyes and blond hair. It could already raise its head. I thought this was a great achievement and was very pleased about it. I told my mother and Michael to look, but they weren't pleased as I was and just stood there mute."

Dreams of Maria's Mother
"I was holding a naked, crying baby in my hands. I don't know where he came from. I looked around a little uncertainly. Before me stood two old Italian women. 'Where does the child come from?' I asked them. They both shook their heads back and forth and said softly, 'It belongs to no one.' A third woman stepped up, somewhat energetic, small, plump, with a toothless mouth. 'So,' she said, 'look carefully at the baby; then you will see that you yourself are the child.' "

"I gave birth to all six of our children at one time. They were so delightfully small that I could hold three in each arm. Each of them had real cat's ears instead of normal ears. I should bite off their little ears so that they would all someday be independent in life. But I couldn't bring myself to do it."

Maria's Dream
(From the same month, which the mother heard directly from Maria and passed on to me):
"My mother had a blond baby, but disowned it. Then she had one with black eyes, and this one she accepted."

This rich family of children made me, as well as the dreamers, happy; but then, I somehow had a part in the begetting. Too, the dreams were given to me in somewhat the way that a woman 'gives her husband a child.' Interestingly, both the first two children came on the day before Christmas, the day of Christ's birth. I could lightheartedly play the roles of both progenitor and King which Maria and her mother transferred to me, because I understood them to be not personal, but rather supra-personal. The therapy stands in place of an inner authority of the patients, a 'Self', which timidly and tentatively tries to become a reality. The great affection felt for 'Doctor' expresses the joy of having come closer to this Self, with the help of the therapeutic companion, it is true, but above all with the help of the dreams and other wellsprings from the unconscious.

That the child is her very own, and thus a birth of her Self, is shown in the dream of the mother, in which she has to recognize herself in the newborn. Such a newborn child carries the possibility within itself of beginning again from the beginning, under new, freer conditions. But it also brings the responsibility with it of caring for this child. For now its wellbeing is entirely under the control of the ego, the dreamer, who can no longer refer back to evil step-parents or such like. Now it has become a personal responsibility, which is indeed why Maria finds her baby on her 'homework desk'.

Maria fell in love with an Italian, and with him discovered her inclination toward southern gaiety and freedom. From one side, this set her provocatively against her mother, who was so ashamed of this background. But she also had another, most likely unconscious, need to reawaken this neglected heritage in her mother. Once she took her mother by the hand and showed her an Italian dance, which her mother enjoyed. How interesting, that in her dream she had her mother give birth to a black-eyed child! She herself, in contrast, gives life to a blue-eyed baby, who, moreover, already raises its head (very early!). Here, as well, the compensatory function of the dream is at work: the mother is to accept the easygoing Italian blood in herself; Maria, on the other hand, her Germanic competence. To each belongs that which she had neglected up till now.

Bewitchment

That Maria and her mother time after time dream of one another, even for one another, testifies to their deep inner attachment and fusion (*participation mystique*), which calls for dissolution and liberation. It was for this reason that I could understand so well that Maria vehemently tore herself from her mother, and that the mother had to disown her daughter. One could not expect that in Maria's baby dream the mother would be pleased about the baby. To the contrary, the witch must burn the stepdaughter, and the latter must, in her turn, united with her king, throw the witch into the fire. Who is the witch, and who the bride, I would like to leave open. Each of them, Maria and mother alike, is striving for the further unfolding of her Self, or, in the language of the fairy tale, toward rulership over the kingdom. Really, both are both, and each uses the other for the projection of her inner archetypal images.

In Maria's dreams witches appear as follows:

Witch-Dreams

"*We (the whole family) went on a trip to a village. We saw farmhouses like those next door to us at home. There was an old house with spiderwebs . . . I wanted to look inside. Then a strange, pale woman came to the door. We became afraid and all ran away; I was last. My mother couldn't run so fast and slowed me down. The old woman had cast a spell on us: 'Now you must sleep 50 years, until so and so many threads have been woven on the loom.'*"

"*I went into a store which was in the woods. I wanted to have a blue-and-white checked bed cover. The woman gave me a brown-and-white one. I first noticed the mistake outside, but I took the cover back immediately, asking for the right one. Then she gave me the right material, but only as big as a dishcloth. Again I gave it back and went out, and then I felt that this woman was a witch. I became afraid. Later I went back there again, with Rosemarie. All the fabrics had disappeared. Rosemarie also felt immediately that she was a witch. She could also do magic. On the way home I found a knife in the snow, with which I could fight against the witch, for she was very evil and sinister. In my fear I prayed as I went back there again. As I confronted the witch I asked definitely and surely for the bed cover. My fear had entirely disappeared."*

Felix and Christian were telling about an extremely strange woman who lived in a big cave. She could also do magic. Everyone close to this woman was asleep; I was very afraid and stayed close to the exit. In this cave one could select eyeglasses. Michael put on a pair, but they didn't especially suit him. I found a pair which didn't suit me, either. Elsbeth desperately wanted Michael's pair. The cave passages led inward in a spiral shape, with a few turn-offs. Felix repeatedly said that I should go inside once to the woman, that she would certainly do nothing to me. The others had just come from her. I came into a room where it was pitch black. Despite the fact that one could see absolutely nothing, I sensed that the woman was there. I felt a great panic, the fear nearly overwhelmed me, I had an indescribable feeling, screamed and ran out of there."

Mother's Dream (from her childhood)
"When I wanted to go to my parents at the apartment, the same witch always opened the door to me in very friendly fashion, but then grabbed me, tickled and pinched me violently, and pulled me down the cellar stairs into the same corner and said, 'I am your father's witch' (father had a lover in addition to his wife). She left me lying there each time. Full of fear, I wanted to call my parents. I never did it, though; I knew that they wouldn't hear me and would not come to free me, either."

Common to these encounters with witches is that they are associated with fear. Maria is accompanied each time, be it by the family, a friend or by her (or at least the two oldest) siblings. For the mother it is a dreadful, lonely experience. The meaning of

Maria's first witch dream is associated with the family history (the wish and importance for the family to experience a renewal). In the second she dares a direct confrontation with the witch, and the astonishing change follows immediately. The third dream seems to me to portray a rite of initiation (maturation ceremonial). The whole ritual reminds me of the custom of an African tribe. The details have several typical characteristics of such rites: the darkness, the panicky fear, the aura of the numinous, the labyrinthine arrangement, the ordeal-like character of the entire act, possibly the instruction by an old woman (cf. with Martin: the wise old man).

When the strange woman can do magic, she becomes capable of creating change or transformation, which is precisely the goal of an initiation. At the same time, going into the cave is a regression into a place of primal security. Maria is ambivalent toward this step. Her little brother gives her the last impetus. The glasses help the eyes of each one they fit to gain a new view of things. The "spiral inward-leading cave passages" may well lead, like a snail shell, round and round, ever closer to the middle, to the "strange woman". It is a task of initiation to sleep near this woman, in the sense of leading to a deeper Self-encounter. The other dream, with fifty years passing during the act of weaving, hints at a similar contemplative deepening which the initiates have to experience. Sleeping in the temple in ancient Greece made this archetypal pattern a solid institution.

In Maria's mother's dream the destructive witchiness is more in evidence. It was uncertain to me whether it was not an entirely concrete family situation which was involved here, perhaps a psychic, if not physical, abuse of the child. Seen psychologically, the archetypal image of the "witch" had to take on a real-life form, since working with this complex on a personal, psychic level had not been attempted or was impossible. The liberation from the ghost had not yet taken place. And so this woman still had to battle with the "witch", who opposed her in the form of the evil mother-in-law, among others.

Transformation

After the time of the witch dreams, Maria was another person. She also faced me with certainty, just as she had the witch. To me, it was as if she had been awakened from a 50-years' sleep. Now she could tell me her opinions and desires clearly and openly. In school—the school term would end in a few weeks—she gave up her resigned passivity. And she was looking forward to a training period as a volunteer in a hospital (after which she failed to pass an entrance examination for training as a medical assistant—she was not up to the testing pressure, especially in working with a stopwatch).

Her transference toward me during this time underwent a change as well. My time as 'King' had run out; for her I no longer had great magical power. This was a sobering experience for both of us, but it also brought about a great gain for Maria: she had now discovered some of the royal power in herself. She wrote me in a letter that she had always expected that I would notice, or know, why she was the way she was, and that I would help her. Yet now she realized that this was impossible. She also wrote that she now understood that the figures in her dreams and fantasies were a part of her self. She still often felt torn between contradictory moods; sometimes she wanted to wreck everything and just lose control again. It seemed to me, though, that she had gained mastery over these various 'people' in herself.

We do not want to forget 'Brother and Sister', but rather look to see where Maria now found herself on her developmental path. But here I must make another basic remark about the dynamics of dreams and fairy tales. The deep relationship between dreams and fairy tales as mediators of the personal and collective unconscious has become clear from Maria's dreams. In fairy tales, as in dreams, the rules of space and time lose their strict and narrow validity. As we have seen, the dream figures are also ambiguous and cannot be neatly assigned to particular figures in outer reality. Developmental steps which manifest themselves in the dream are not taken so clearly in outer life; they may lag temporarily behind or extend themselves over a longer time than the ideal, text-book dream presentation would lead us to suppose. For this reason my readers, too, will find a few uncertainties about the temporal-logical co-ordination between inner and outer lines of development.

I, too, had to experience over and over in my work with Maria and her mother the fact that, despite the 'breakthroughs' in the dreams, 'relapses' are possible, indeed are necessary, for without them the new achievements are lost. Many energies which announced themselves in dreams came to their final unfolding for the first time years later. It was as if the two women were to keep the power of these dreams in a treasure chest, so that they would be available in due course.

'Sister' as the queen met her death in the mortal heat of the fiery bath which the jealous stepmother had prepared for her. Was that true for Maria and her mother? Yes; the mother's jealousy was overpowering. And just as overpowering was her hot maternal love. This 'killing' also took place on another level, though: in her dream Maria, together with her whole family, falls into a 50-years' sleep near the witch. Among the ancient Greeks one spoke of sleep (Hypnos) as the younger brother of death (Thanatos); a sleep of 50 years would then be nearly an 'older brother'! Similarly, in the cave dream those coming into the domain of the "strange woman" fall into sleep, and to encounter this woman brings panicky fear, as if she were deadly. And we find a similar pattern also in the mother's childhood dream: she is in the cellar, under the power of the horrible witch, imprisoned and cut off from everything familiar and dear to her, as though she were dead.

The dramatic plan of the fairy tale demands our respect. It follows laws which are beyond human influence. The ancient experience of mankind is contained in the fairy tale in condensed form. In the therapy with these two women I tried to impart to them this deep respect for archetypal events. This meant as well that we had to recognize such emotions as jealousy, 'evil', and rage as an expression of this higher law. In the dynamics of the fairly tale are even requirements for the ongoing process, which lead to healing and a happy ending. It was, on the other hand, the dreams themselves which supported the clash with the hidden powers, as in the encounter with the animal within. Through such encounters 'evil' powers were redeemed and could develop their creative effects.

Something must die, so that something new can awaken. This is an experience which every crisis we truly go through teaches us.

The crisis at puberty seems to me to be an especially memorable model and teaching example. In this regard pubescent children can become invaluable teachers for their parents. Crises therefore should and must occur. Efforts to mitigate or even avert a crisis are wrong. Parents have a part in the crisis, and for this reason we should not expect them to stand above it and observe everything only rationally and reasonably. Rather they can and should make 'mistakes', which in retrospect will prove to be absolutely right.

Especially with respect to Maria, for example, the parents were right to declare their daughter to be virtually dead, 'written off'. In this way the process could take its course in the spirit of the fairy tale. With the other children the parents had not been able to let go in the same way. Today it has come about that the former problem child, Maria, who made her own way, has become a leadership figure in the family. In one of the mother's later dreams Maria appeared as an orchestra conductor! There was also a dream from Maria (see above, pages 36–37) in which she asked her mother to abandon her continual, anxious control and instead to let things run their course. The dream says that she should keep silent, so that her 'scream of fear' does not disturb Felix as he is swimming. We were reminded of the proverbial 'sure-footed sleepwalker', an example of that instinctive, spontaneous activity which must not be interrupted by too much control.

While I encouraged the mother to let matters take their course, for Maria I had to be both leader and companion during the darkest period. I had to give her courage to keep going on through the "spiral-shaped cave passages", despite the "panicky fear" with which she would truly go through the symbolic death. This meant in daily life that I accepted her depression, the blackness of her mood, as necessary along her way. I did not try to cheer her up and thus divert her from the path toward maturity. In this situation it was probably vital that Maria had had such a high opinion of me and projected onto me the 'King', who from his castle had both perspective and overview. The moment she came to the end of the path through the darkness, I again became for her an ordinary human being.

◇ ◇ ◇ ◇ ◇ ◇ ◇ ◇ ◇ ◇ ◇

Redemption

I would like now to look into the 're-awakening to new life'. In the fairy tale the king recognizes the voice of his wife. It is because he answers her that she becomes alive again, once more flesh and blood. Did I as 'King' do justice to this task? Did I recognize the mysterious voice which could be heard from, so to speak, the other side? And did I answer, did I make my self answerable to it? Maria herself filled our hours with eternal silence. It was with her dreams that she 'spoke' to me. Each time I asked her for them, she handed them to me with an air of deep significance and tacit consent. My willing ear for this language was essential to her. Once I refrained from asking her the almost-ritual question about her dreams. In her pocket she had the very meaningful dream of the witch's cave ready for me. Later I asked her why she had withheld this dream from me. She replied, "But you didn't ask for it!" This was an important lesson for me. I was still her 'King', her larger ego, which had to ask, understand, and answer for her.

Only gradually did the 'King' in her grow, that is to say, her consciousness of her own responsibility for herself and her own path. In the letter previously referred to there was already a hint of this. In the end it is a question of 'Know Thyself!'—the motto of the Oracle at Delphi.

It is now about time to burn the witch, if we wish to keep to the chronological order of the fairy tale. As I have already intimated, the neat structure, the orderly sequence of events in the fairy tale, is not to be taken literally or applied so explicitly to reality. The various developmental steps which are so vividly portrayed in the fairy tale are complexly interwoven in Maria's life. The burning of the witch takes place at the moment in which Maria boldly faces her mother with new self-awareness. In the dream she armed herself with a knife as a precaution, before she "definitely and surely . . . confronted" the witch. And at that point "the fear had completely disappeared". To look the witch in the eyes means to clash with her. Maria had already learned that this would be a confrontation with her own witch inside, for it was, really, her dream. The same was true with respect to her mother, in whom she experienced and confronted her inner witch image. Who is not familiar with this phenomenon: when we finally overcome our fears and confront our most dreaded adversary, each of us seems suddenly changed.

The fire in which the witch burns corresponds to the fire in us, which drives us to action and to confrontation. Looked at psychologically as well as chemically, burning is a process of transformation to a new state. By critically looking at one's shadow side, the shadow takes on a different color, and one even discovers valuable, hidden (personal) qualities in it. In Jungian psychology we speak of the integration of the shadow. It is an important step along the way to personal wholeness, the path which we call becoming one's Self or 'Individuation'.

The witch is burned, the ghost is gone, life can go on. It was refreshing for me to see how independently Maria could relate to her mother. The parental expectations, especially with regard to her profession, didn't concern her any longer, and for this reason she did not have to rebel against them any more. She decided to 'go out into the wide world' and wait for what was in store for her. The mother no longer had her daughter and her daughter's life path 'firmly in hand', as she had continually tried to manage it up till now, at the expense of all her energy. At first she felt that she had been deprived of her power and driven into a corner. In her role as witch she had been killed.

A Dream of Maria's Mother
"From the very top of a high tower, I looked out a window
down to the courtyard. There the hands of some prisoners of
war were being tied together. 'Dreadful,' I thought, 'they are
captured, robbed of their freedom.' I went into a real rage. I
took a long knife and ran down the stairs. It was up to me, as
there was no sign of it stopping. Finally I was in the
courtyard. I quickly cut through all the chains. The last one
said, 'What you did helped us to our freedom, but yours is
over. Escape, as fast as you can!' I let the knife fall. Haunted
by fear, I ran across the square. I called behind me, 'I want
my freedom and more.' From far away I heard called back to
me: 'That you'll never have.'"

She gives freedom and loses freedom. The dream stresses again that, as a result of the freedom of her escaping children, she is thrown back onto herself, is in prison, where she must now 'do her time'. Does she have secret guilt feelings? Or is it the prison of her own childhood?

Once again Maria proves to be a pioneer, for the mother, as well:

A Dream of the Mother
"Maria stood triumphantly before me. She grew ever taller,
and I became ever smaller. The shrinking hurt very much. I
looked backwards. 'Soon I will arrive at my childhood.' It
went on; I was seized with fear. I fought and set myself
against it. It didn't help. Suddenly everything stood still.
Before me lay an endless plain, barrenness and loneliness. I
looked for people, flowers, trees and animals, to no avail.
Someone pushed me from behind. I shouted, 'No, not a single
step can I take into this region!' Again I looked around me. I
wanted to flee, but to which side? Everything was far away
from me, frightening!"

Both of us, she and I, were very grateful for this dream. It accurately described the new situation in a nutshell, captured the entire dynamics and, moreover, offered the link to her way forward. At the beginning of the dream we see how the growth of her daughter painfully upset her. This dream, like many others, tries to correct, to compensate for, a one-sided conscious attitude by particularly emphasizing the opposite. This means here that the dreamer is challenged to place her underestimated daughter in a higher position and put herself correspondingly lower. With this she is literally thrown back onto herself, against which she has fought for a long time and which she continues to fight. The following night she dreamed that she wanted to put up storm windows to keep the children from leaving the nest. This angry, backward look was unavoidable. She had to make peace with her childhood in order to be able to look further and forward.

The freedom which resulted from this was astonishing, boundless, even uncanny. A blank page lay before her. It was as if she had to recreate the whole world. In this dream, flowers, trees, animals and people were missing. Seeing this provided a great creative incentive for her. I see her yet before me, how she rolled her sleeves up and worked in her garden, planted vegetables, kept rabbits and ducks. Here, too, there was a restlessness, a necessity. This new creative impulse was a blessing for the children, for it allowed them to escape their mother's manipulative gaze and go their own ways.

At that time the oldest son, Michael, said that his mother was behaving as if she were at the beginning of puberty. When I steered the conversation toward the years of her youth, she broke into tears—she could say nothing more about this time which weighed so heavily on her. I had the feeling that I must go with this woman through her hellfire. It was amazing how calmly she could soon let her children develop in freedom. I felt a pleasant radiance from her, as well. She seemed to me to be completely redeemed. She realized that it was Maria who, precisely through her 'disgusting' behavior toward her mother, had contributed to the redemption of the 'witch' within her mother.

It did not surprise me that she could now see her own 'evil' mother in an entirely new light. Her new projections onto this mother had at times even an aura of the 'old wise woman'—corresponding to the change which she herself had inwardly experienced. In the eyes of her mother, Maria, too, was completely changed. When she now and then appeared at home, between her comings and goings in the world, her mother experienced her as grown-up and mature. Maria also had something to give. She taught her mother to dance, but at the same time forced her to open her eyes to the dark sides of the world, drugs, sex and youth problems, which up till now had been submerged in the all too heathy climate of the family. When the mother told me now about Maria, it sounded as though she was speaking about a sister ('Brother and Sister'!).

How beautifully that fit into the logic of the fairy tale! The witch is dead, the little brother has been saved. What could be more obvious than to assume that the two transformations are closely tied to each other, that in the soul of the mother there is now room for a brotherly heart in place of the witch who has been driven out? Viewed intrapsychically, subjectively, Maria had now become a good brother to herself, in that she treated herself as protectively and supportively as had her big brother, to whom she had been so closely attached. I, too, came to feel the brotherly element, when she—albeit years later—saw me as a big brother, and no longer the 'King'.

What Happened Afterwards

After Maria went on her travels, she stayed in contact with me by letter. Altogether I received twelve letters from her. She had to go 'through thick and thin' away from home, too. She came to sense the harshness of life 'outside'. Both a bit of homesickness and the distance helped her to see her parents and the family in a new light and to view them more calmly.

The mother continued her therapy with me quite a while longer, four years in all. She still fell into many 'holes' in her search for freedom and a middle ground between her inner opposites. But there came a time when I also heard from her, 'I did it!' With that she meant above all getting over her problems with her mother-in-law, who had lain for so long like a big stumbling-block in her path. And for her it was a small triumph that she could now enjoy being alone with me in therapy, no longer just the 'witch', but rather the 'King's bride'.

Maria, in the meantime, travelled all over the place under her own steam. She spent a few months as an assistant in a home for special education, then she settled with a group of young people somewhere in France on a river lock, then with a friend on a mountain in the Alps, always living very simply. Her plan to train in special education fell through. But above all, she wanted to remain free and not submit herself to new, constricting obligations, since those from her schooldays and childhood still troubled her.

Recently she visited me again and brought me up to date on things. Today she is working as an assistant in a home for the elderly. There she learned pedicure, which she might someday practice at home. She is in the fourth month of pregnancy, and is delighted about the baby. Her friend, with whom she shares a small apartment, is studying to be a psychiatric worker. He loves her deeply, and she too cannot imagine living with anyone else. She still feels a little confined by the thought of marriage, but the two of them have now decided to marry. I enjoyed her radiant openness as she spoke. She has become a balanced and beautiful woman!

After I had again, so many years later, absorbed myself in the moving story of Maria and her mother and tried to bring their lives' paths into interrelationship, I wanted to invite them to both join me in a discussion. I also had to obtain their agreement to lift the veil from their secrets, which up till now I had strictly kept in the custody of my 'safe'. And each of them had the right to keep her secrets from the other.

They both came, the mother immediately and gladly, Maria a bit hesitantly, for she felt very exposed in the presence of her mother in this way. They came laughing to see me, partly out of embarrassment, partly for the joy of reunion. In reaction to the old memories, Maria suddenly felt confined and hot, and had to spend some time out in the garden, while her mother took the opportunity to pour out her heart. It is true that the mother-in-law is dead, but she still dreams of her from time to time as though she were still alive. And an aged neighbor woman now has exactly the same kind of relationship to her husband as did the mother-in-law; it drives her to despair. Maria finds it a great relief to realize that her mother had projected her own fundamental problems onto her.

As she said goodbye, Maria radiantly handed me the invitation to her wedding.

Martin

Background

In the days around Easter a minister called me: there was a young man in his confirmation class who was causing him a lot of worry. Recently he had refused to take part in the confirmation ceremony, and instead remained seated, silent and depressed, in the background. He was not the sort of rebellious boy who makes fun of the church and its forms; on the contrary, he was a particularly thoughtful, quiet young man struggling with his inner problems. During the preparations for confirmation he showed how seriously he took the matter. The minister stressed to me that he tried as far as possible to accommodate the 'modern trends' among young people, in order not to 'shock' them with outmoded ceremonial. For the celebration in church they were allowed to dress as they liked, and the whole was structured as 'painlessly' as possible, that is to say, without a lot of fuss. And so he was all the more astonished at the way this young man reacted.

I invited Martin's entire family to a first discussion in my psychiatric practice, both in order to familiarize myself with the youngster's surroundings, and also to win the family over to the forthcoming work. Martin was large for his age of 15; in his physical and sexual development he was already a mature man. But as his mother described him to me as "our young man", he contradicted her amazingly fiercely: but he is their child, just like always! He gave an impression of silent despair. His inhibited movements seemed to express how cramped and imprisoned he must have felt, by outer as well as inner conflicts.

In the 'City Test' (after Baudouin) Martin was given the task of combining eight different public municipal buildings into one picture (Figure 1). The school occupies a central position in his drawing. It lies closely hemmed in by a mountain, a fence, a high-tension wire and a closed railroad barrier. The city is devoid of people. The sky shows a transition from clear to darkly cloudy, from left to right. On each side there is a mountain: on the left, under the clear sky, stands a church; on the right, under the dark clouds, a castle.

Figure 8 *City Test (drawing)*

The church (*mater ecclesia*: Mother Church) possibly reflects his personal view of his mother, who had recently, for the sake of her husband, converted to the Catholic church in a search for meaning in the religious. The beautiful weather over the 'Mother' may be an expression of the carefree world of childhood which Martin was still looking for from his mother. The black clouds from the factory, however, already darken the sky before her.

The towering castle on the mountain, above right, reminded me of the over-glorifying description Martin gave of his father, whose demands for performance he must have experienced as inhuman. The dark clouds could represent the depressive crises which even at that time seemed to be increasingly threatening over his father. His father had become unreachable to him: the way to the castle becomes lost in the forest. In short, as he himself said, "Something's gone wrong in my relationship with my father!" On closer examination I recognized a branching yellow signpost at the fork in the road on the mountain. Martin appears to stand here before an important decision: Shall he pursue the steep, partially hidden path which leads up to the grey castle, or shall he take the level, short path which leads straight to the cemetery? With some feelings of uneasiness I connected this short road to Martin's recent hints at suicide. They led me to fear that the peace of the graveyard was not only meant symbolically but could be a real possibility for him.

The Family

Figure 9 *The Family as Animals I (drawing)*

In his 'Family as Animals' (a popular test in psychiatric practice with children and adolescents), Martin paints an impressive portrait of the dynamics in his family. All the members are deep under water on the sea floor, in the realm of the deep unconscious, if we may understand the water in this way. He himself is a many-colored fish. Five bubbles hint at his relationship with the element of air, which stands closer to the spiritual and to consciousness than does water. Close above him in a menacing position we see his father as an electric eel. The red streaks—so goes his zoological explanation—portray the electricity which this animal gives off. An opponent is paralyzed by it. I learned that the father was an engineer with the railroad. Is there not something of the electrically-driven power of an express train in the appearance of this animal? Building an electric train set-up was for many years an attractive common interest between father and son. "My father can always do everything better; he was always the great example"—nearly overpowering, as it appears also in this picture. But for a year Martin had felt that "between my father and me something is wrong." His father gave him presents, many of which he would rather not have received, and no wonder: the 'gift' which an electric eel has to give is paralyzing and not conducive to one's personal progress. The father also felt envious and jealous, since his son was able to go to high school and acted as if he were his mother's bridegroom.

We see Martin's mother at the edge of the picture, lower right, as a jellyfish, smiling stupidly to herself. She herself was permitted to see this drawing and said, "Oh, yes, I know, I hold onto my son with my thousand arms!" After the birth of her first child (Martin) she had had a "great feeling of happiness", while the father seemed to be caught in his own existential fears and was hardly available to the family due to his additional studies. And so the mother took possession of their son all the more: "I have invested everything in him." Before he was eleven years old he could not let his mother go out because of his fears of abandonment. But since then, the mother complained, she could no longer really get close to him. On the other hand, as I heard it, Martin looked for refuge in his mother's bed at night, when he was tormented by indescribable, mortal fears. He gives his brother Daniel, two years younger, the form of a seahorse, which here seems childishly playful and carefree.

Martin's situation seemed desperate. His family portrait graphically confirmed the hopeless problem. It was clear to all of us that 'something must happen'! I gave him a medical excuse for school and prescribed, as a temporary, less-than-ideal solution, an antidepressive medication. In order to give his free time at home content and meaning, I instructed him to paint a picture every day and to bring them with him to the therapeutic hours. In addition he had the task of writing a diary. This whole arrangement gave him a sort of security and hope.

Depression

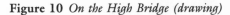

Figure 10 *On the High Bridge (drawing)*

In this picture (Figure 10), the two complementary colors orange and purple collide powerfully with one another, like an intensification of the weather-mood contrasts in Martin's first picture. Martin gave his own commentary on this spontaneous drawing: "I am standing on the high bridge; below me it goes dreadfully far down. After the bridge the path divides. My path leads down into the tunnel under the castle. In front of the entrance to the tunnel is a dangerous abyss. The tunnel is long and dark . . ." In a later reflection on the picture Martin thought that at the very end of the tunnel the light returns. At first it could only be seen as a point.

The way from left to right leads from the light into the darkness, from the known into the unknown. Is it the path out of maternal security into the cruelly demanding world of the father?

The fair weather over the mother-church in the first picture increases here on the left side of the drawing into a glowing heat which could nearly burn someone. We suspect the conflict which

75

Martin must suffer with respect to his mother: she has a thousand arms, as she herself acknowledged. Flight from her clutching and overheating seems imperative.

An atmosphere of mystery hangs in this sky. Elemental forces are constellating and contrasting with each other. There are higher powers involved, which express themselves in Martin's picture and which go far beyond his personal mother and personal father: the archetype of the Mother is confronting that of the Father. Collective human experiences find their expression here.

The Great Father shows itself here as an unshakable principle. One senses an Olympian father, whose thunder rolls through sinister heavens. As an earthly mortal, one cannot stand face to face with him. There remains only the path underneath and through to overcome him. On the other side the Great Mother threatens, first in the form of the 'hot' sky, but also in the form of the deep chasm into which one may crash. Complete security in a "primal unitary reality" (Erich Neumann) with the mother is at the same time a threat to one who strives toward consciousness. Excessive security is accompanied by the loss of new consciousness, and is experienced by the growing man as 'being burned' or as a threatening 'crash into the depths,' that is, the deep unconscious (or perhaps even as a 'crash into psychosis'!).

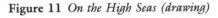

Figure 11 *On the High Seas (drawing)*

Figure 11 gives us a glimpse of the inner experiences which Martin had to undergo at this time: the man is in great distress after falling out of his boat. From one side a huge wave threatens to break over him, from the other a devouring sea monster approaches. Luckily, as Martin explains to me, at just the right time the little sailor was able to jam an oar in the fish's mouth to keep his way out clear, "just in case." It is a blessing that in this dangerous situation the sun stretches a rescuing hand out to the drowning man. "How nice it is when someone thinks of you!" he said the same day, when he received a greeting card from his minister.

What Martin did not know, however, was that the contents of his picture—or was it a dream?—seem to be a nearly exact reproduction of a Polynesian myth. The hero, along with his boat, is swallowed up by a sea monster, but sticks the mast of his boat in the mouth of the beast beforehand in order to keep it open. After that he slides into the depths of the belly, where he rediscovers his (deceased) parents. He makes a fire, kills the monster, and gets out again through the open jaws. This myth provides the directions for a ceremonial test of manhood, an initiation rite, as it is still performed today in the Polynesian area. The monster there may be made out of paper, but that takes nothing away from the initiates' dreadful fears during this ceremony.

In his deep despair and crisis, Martin had come into contact with levels of the unconscious which go far beyond his personal experience and that of his family, and which reflect ancient and universally valid human knowledge. The devouring monster is an achetypal pattern, which appears again and again in myths and fairly tales of many times and peoples. And obviously there was also something true and essential in it for Martin, who had never heard such a story. It was an inner experience, which on the one hand underlay and clearly communicated his distress, and which on the other had a place in a larger framework. He learned that his suffering was subject to age-old laws. This awareness alone can be comforting, for one is not completely alone with his fate. Moreover, the picture gives advance notice of the rescuer: the sun offers a hand. And in the myth, at the end the hero steps back out of the belly of the monster and into the light as a changed man.

Martin's thoughts and fantasies in the next days and weeks were devoted to memories of his unalloyed, secure childhood. Many dreams, however, foretold a danger from the new and unknown, like storm clouds. In one dream he sought "cover in the berth of a (ship's) cabin . . . unfortunately without a teddy bear", while the war raged outside in the cold and snow. His nursing of his childish needs appeared to be like a summoning-up of powers in the face of difficult new tasks, a step backward in preparation for a more determined move forward. The path to the outside seemed more and more unavoidable, but Martin urgently needed a guiding hand, a light, a spiritual orientation. The sun in his drawing of the drowning man helped me to convey this orientation to him. His path leads through dangerous border experiences; the engulfment by the ocean wave, a symbol of the currents of the deep unconscious, is experienced as a death by drowning. The picture positively cries for the light of a new consciousness. Sometimes Martin came to his hour with me with the fantasy that the way to therapy was like swimming a great sea, and each time he barely made it between panicky attacks of breathlessness. Here, too, is the fear of being engulfed by water, and the fear of running out of air (consciousness?).

Breakout

Dream
*"I had a gigantic festering tooth in my mouth. I couldn't close
my mouth any more. Only with great difficulty did I manage
to knock out this firmly-rooted tooth. The pus dripped out and
filled an entire bowl. Then I suddenly had completely normal
teeth in my mouth again."*

Imagine having such a handicap in one's own mouth . . . that
must hurt! It hinders the taking of nourishment as well as speech.
Irrespective of what origin this 'festering tooth' has in Martin's
life, how fortunate it is that in his dream Martin finds the
strength to rid himself of this burden!

In certain rites of initiation it is the custom to break an incisor
tooth out of the initiate's mouth, presumably a last relic of an ancient myth, in which the young man is cut and burned in order to
prepare him for a new life. It seems to me that a part of this age-
old human knowledge is discernible in Martin's dream.

There followed more days and nights of dramatic despair and
deathly fears of school, until he discovered that school is really
the extended arm of the father, which he had to ruthlessly tackle
as never before. New life was also perceptible when Martin said it
was "enough to drive me up the wall", "thoughts flash through my
head like lightning", or "it's as if my head is occupied by strange
figures."

At the end of a sandplay (figure 12), on which he had concen-
trated intently, he gave me (roughly) the following explanation:

> In this city everything is very orderly. Many people live there,
> but they feel lonely. Here and there are small battles at the edges
> of the city. The people are drowning in their problems. There by
> the bridge the cars are crowding out of the city into freedom.
> For the animals outside it's like an attack. The men there in the
> red uniforms are park rangers; they don't notice anything.
> There on the left, behind the thick forest, man and nature live
> peacefully together.

Figure 12 *Breakout from the City (sandplay)*

As in the dream of the festering tooth, something is breaking out here, too. Old constraints are being thrown off, dammed-up powers are being loosed. For once we look directly at this unbridled strength, which appears in person at the exit from the city! These are not Sunday strollers who seek the quiet of nature. No, the urge to get into nature is so overpowering that it is in danger of being overrun and destroyed. Only later, or rather, farther on, is there an area where these opposites get along with each other. The vision of peaceful relations between culture and nature can be understood on the one hand as completely objective, but can also indicate symbolically that stage of maturity where the deep, personal instinctive nature fits in with the adaptation of the adult personality. I had to listen to Martin very carefully to catch these clues, for even the slightest suggestion of something instinctual would recede in view of his parents' powerful moralistic ideas. Questions about sexuality remained unasked and unlived for a long time. All the same, the dream of the festering tooth and this sandplay scene indicate such eruptions. The power which was accumulating within seemed so immense and threatening that Martin's caution in his outer life was all too understandable.

Dream
"I was playing with some household machine. I burned my
hand with it and so had a red spot on my hand. I am in

school, and now the teacher asks me what's wrong with my hand. I show him and see to my astonishment that all of a sudden, it's bleeding. The teacher agrees to fix up the wound. But instead of doing something, he first examines my hand carefully. Then he takes a pencil and runs it around the wound. He says it's not bleeding any more. And when I look at my hand again I notice that something is written on it in my blood; it is bright red, in an old-fashioned handwriting."

Martin connected the contents of this dream with his experience of the therapeutic hours. It is true that no blood flows there. But the work upset him so much that it was as if it were written in his blood on his hand. And again the events go far beyond his personal life: the "old-fashioned handwriting" points to natural laws. Blood plays a central role in rites of initiation. The bleeding wound—in ritual scarification, for example—symbolizes a death or means that the woman-blood is flowing out of the young man to make room for new man-blood. Another view points to the womb-envy of the man, who can understand the experiences of menstruation and birth through the bloody ceremony.

Separation and Loneliness

Dream

*"Apartment wrecking: I broke through a paper wall from a
stage. Behind it there was an apartment. A woman was there,
too. At first I thought she was my wife, but then again it was
some housewife, or rather an old mother-image of mine. She
tried to calm me down and ran behind me. I was in a great
rage. I threw everything I got my hands on onto the floor. In
short, I caused dreadful havoc. The woman implored me to
stop. But I went on. Now, though, I had no more reason to
destroy everything. Nevertheless it gave me pleasure to be able
once to just smash everything. And so I went on, despite the
fact that the woman was nearly in tears."*

With his so well-mannered upbringing and his willingness to
adapt, Martin did not like to read such things in his dream book,
but he was also a bit amused, indeed refreshed, that such rushes
of emotion are possible. Gradually some of this emotion surfaced
in his daily conduct, in his dealings with his mother, or his
teachers—or perhaps the teacher in him, who behaved so com-
pulsively, could never relax or 'look the other way'. He was now
being prepared for a step toward the necessary separation from
his mother: he was not the outcast, as he experienced it up until
now, but instead *he* was pushing his mother from him.

We read that in their ritual of separation the Hottentots make
it virtually a duty for the adolescents to abuse and mistreat their
mothers, so that they can emancipate themselves. In another
tribe the youths becoming men should pour water over their
mothers, after they have asked for it, so that the mothers—so the
rite goes—retreat to their village. How much easier would be the
separation of son from mother and mother from son in our culture, if we had binding collective customs of this sort! Is it not
also precisely this transpersonal, archetypal aspect—Martin describes it in his dream so aptly with 'mother-image'—which can
relativize the personal, perhaps even culpable consternation of a

son or a mother? What can the real mother do about it? It is really about the mother-image which dwells inside the young man. And what can the son do about it? It is in fact a collectively-established pattern, deep within, which he must follow. (As we have seen, this step must also be risked between mother and daughter, if it is to lead to a 'normal' separation.)

Accepting this dream, that is to say, acknowledging its radical contents as a piece of himself, gave Martin a feeling of great liberation also in his daily life. His mortal fear of school gave way to a mere aversion to it. Instead of tormenting worries about his parents I heard about rebellion and the wish to decide his life himself. "I did it ... I could embrace the world!" was written—somewhat pathetically—in his diary. In fact he seemed to have crossed a fundamental threshold. He felt undreamt-of powers in himself: "I want to go away . . ., destroy my neighborhood, with a lightning-bolt . . ." From then on I heard little more of the self-pity which had been so familiar to me. The way was clearing for new developments.

Sandplay has proven to be a wonderful alternative for making the mysterious and inexpressible vividly visible and communicable. Martin, who felt an inner pressure to say many things—often without finding the words for them—gratefully adopted this possibility. (Others of his age react at the beginning more disparagingly to such a 'child's toy', but willingly let the sand—'just for the fun of it'—trickle through their fingers, until it 'grabs' them, too.) What materializes in playing with the sand brings out the child in astonishing ways; there is an exciting dialogue between the player and his play, which increasingly becomes a striking expression of his or her inner personality, of his Self. At the same time, however, it also acts to mold and heal the child, especially when an entire series of sandplay scenes accompanies a developmental process.

Martin was completely focussed on making this sand picture; a world opened up to him in it. Unfortunately, we were both going on vacation shortly thereafter for a few weeks. In order to provide a secure framework for his experience, which had seemed so fulfilling to him, I asked him to write a story to go with his sandplay scene. This he did with great care:

> Feng was the son of a farmer and lived on an oasis in the desert until his sixteenth year. He knew only this oasis; of the rest of the world he knew nothing. But as he grew older, he began to ask questions, for example, 'What does it look like outside the

Figure 13 *Desert Journey*

oasis?' The people in the village for the most part had no sympathy for his questions. It had always been this way. They had
no answer for Feng's question.

When he was sixteen years old he decided to go off into the
world. The people in his native village warned him against it,
for the way through the desert into other lands was very arduous. Seldom had anyone come back who had gone away. But
Feng did not allow himself to be intimidated. Something inside
him urged him on to find an answer. He knew that he wanted to
go to the Fount of Wisdom. It was a hot morning when Feng set
out. He sat in a wagon to which two cattle were harnessed. After
he had looked back again for a moment, he drove straight out
into the desert. When he disappeared over the horizon, a few
people in the village shed a tear or two. Then they turned back
to their daily tasks. In the village all was as it had been.

Feng was sad now as he went through the desert. At intervals
posts were rammed into the ground which were to show the
traveller the way. Feng now turned toward them. In the morning
he had started off from home, and now it was already evening
again. After he had looked up at the stars in the sky for a time,
he fell asleep. He spent the night very restlessly. Again and again
he was jolted out of his dreams. Small wonder that he was happy
when morning came.

On the third day Feng began to feel more and more lonely. In
the afternoon he saw a temple to the right. In front of it sat a
monkey-like creature, which stretched out its hand to beg. Feng
stopped his wagon. Then he drove his cattle to the temple so
that they could rest in the shade. He himself went up to the

monkey. It was a good-natured but also mysterious creature. Feng was glad that in his loneliness he had found any living being at all, and decided to stay overnight in that place. He generously shared his evening meal with the monkey. After that the monkey said that he lived there as a hermit in order to protect the temple. For in the area lived the spirit of the little desert man Wan. And truly, as the two sat around a fire towards midnight, they saw the ghost of a man who had perished here in the desert. He sat on a cow which lay, practically dead of exhaustion, on the ground, and he cursed and swore wildly. As dawn broke, the spook stopped. When Feng said goodbye to his new friend, the monkey thanked him for the supper and gave Feng an old book in return. "It will surely be of use to you one day," he said. Then Feng went on. Four days later he saw a wonderfully beautiful house on the horizon. He wanted to turn immediately off the path when he remembered that there are mirages in the desert. They can be the downfall of the lonely traveller, for if he turns toward the mirages, he can easily stray from the path and become lost in the desert. And so Feng tried to orient himself strictly to the path markers which, however, were not always clearly visible.

Several days passed. Feng again felt very lonely. He was slowly losing patience. And patience is something very important for a man.

The path was less and less visible. One day Feng saw something in the distance which jutted out of the sand. He leaped from the wagon and rushed in the direction of the strange object. It was a wagon. Feng could also recognize the skeletons of the draft animals and the driver. Everything was stuck in the sand. This driver had been unlucky. Is that a bad omen for our friend? Feng fell into a panic. What would happen now, if he were also lost in the desert? He would certainly have to share the fate of that unknown driver. He trotted sadly and full of fear back to his wagon. For the whole day, he just stared straight ahead as his draft animals slowly pulled the wagon through the desert.

At night he didn't sleep well. Two days later Feng, who had given up all hope, spotted a point on the horizon. As he came wearily closer to it, he suddenly recognized a column. Chiseled into it were characters which Feng didn't understand. He could only read the sentence which was over them:

To him who can decipher
this writing,
will the path open to the
Fount of Wisdom!

Feng sat on the ground and examined the writing. But he simply could not make out what appeared there.

Thus he stayed two days and two nights; once again he was close to despair. Then he remembered the book that the temple attendant had given him. He brought it out of his baggage, sat down again in front of the column, and opened the book. And behold, he found the meaning of the characters. Slowly he murmured to himself the phrase that was chiseled into the column: "Be careful; you've made it until now, but I cannot give you the answer. Go over this bridge—Good Luck!" Feng looked around, and suddenly he saw a bridge over which there was a path. He climbed onto his wagon and drove it over the bridge. On the other side he unhitched his oxen from the wagon so that they could drink some water. But only one of them stepped into the stream. Hardly had it put its head into the water when a black monster appeared and swallowed up the animal. Feng was intensely afraid. After he had recovered from the shock, he tied his baggage to the remaining draft animal. Then he set off down the path, which led into a valley. He left the empty wagon behind. Feng had never imagined that there would be a valley in the middle of the desert. The route markers had disappeared, and so our little hero had to fight his way through the sand.

On the next day he came to a dam. A castle, whose walls stretched clear across the valley, blocked Feng's path. It is true that there was also a gate, which even stood open, but it was guarded by four wrathful soldiers. Feng became frightened anew. How could he get through this guarded gate? He finally decided to bravely walk up to the gate and ignore the soldiers. As he came closer to them he suddenly saw that they were not really soldiers at all, but only set-up puppets. Feng heaved a sigh of relief. He was very tired. So he decided to rest in the castle. Indeed, he stayed there the entire night. In the morning the chirping of a bird woke him. The happiness of this animal was contagious. Once more, he set off cheerfully on his way. Suddenly there lay before him a green plain with woods and villages. He could also see snow-capped mountains in the background. He leaped into the air. Then he travelled on. For the first time in many days he whistled a song. But no one could tell him where the Fount of Wisdom was. After a few years he gave up the search and settled down in a village near the mountains. He lived there from that time on. He forgot how he came to be there.

One day, as he was walking in the mountains, he met an old man. He sat in front of a hut near a fountain. The old man lived very simply. Feng was surprised at this. Then the old man said: "You are at the goal of your wandering. What do you wish to know?" Feng thought a long time, then said, "Since I am now content, there is nothing I wish to know." "You are correct; contentment is more valuable than wisdom."

Growing Up

That was a hero's tale of an epic character! Wherever did Martin get these images and patterns, which condense all the important steps of initiation into a sort of synopsis? Some of these steps he had already put behind him; others still stood before him but had already been lived as inner experiences, *in nucleo,* like a nutshell.

In absolutely astonishing ways we find these same images when we look into ethnological reports on the rites of the 'primitives'. As they were in Martin, the universally valid, basic patterns of transition seem to be preserved undisturbed. What is given in traditional societies as a ritual frame to the awakening, maturing children is also present in our youth as an archetypal anticipation seeking fulfillment. There are many stop-gaps; with Martin the unfulfilled search led to depression and breakdown, and finally to therapy.

The following basic patterns become apparent in Martin's story just like in the transition rites of primitive peoples: the break with the family; the loneliness; the nearness of death, perhaps a symbolically performed death; a spiritual instruction; the surviving of an ordeal of a physical and spiritual nature; and finally—also symbolically—a new birth. It was amazing to me to find the same rites in ethnological literature that Martin spontaneously laid out, down to the details. In a myth of the Malekula tribe there is a Great Earth Mother who meets the souls of the dead at the entrance to her cave; in front of her is the map of a labyrinth, drawn on the ground. As soon as a seeking soul approaches she covers up half of it. One who knows the map—that is, one who is initiated—finds his way easily; one who does not know it is eaten by the old woman on the spot. Applied to Martin's story, since one of his cattle was pulled down into the depths by the black monster, we can conclude that again half of his energies had to be sacrificed to the unconscious; his initiation into adulthood had only half occurred. For the moment he seemed content with this: "Contentment is more valuable than wisdom," we hear from the mouth of the old man.

Martin had built up his story so lovingly and with such complexity that it was clear to me how very much he was bound up with, indeed even identical with, its far-reaching events. They were a part of him. My task was to hold together the sometimes anxiety-provoking dynamics of these events, to give them a framework; to put it simply: to be close to Martin. My presence seemed important and effective for him, without my doing anything concrete; I was 'only' an attentive, involved companion who 'stuck up for him' on his way and encouraged him to go on. We felt a closeness on both sides which at best can be described as 'participation mystique' (Levy-Brühl). It seemed important that the atmosphere of the archetypal be given space and acknowledgment. The more powerful the experiences, the fewer the words for them. And so we were silent—out of respect for the significance of his inner experience—and we understood each other better in this way than with words. At the same time he demanded that I be also a leader, someone who is sure of his ground and does not let himself be upset by the powerful moods and contents which he brought to therapy. I found it an exhausting task to steer the proper course between these two demands.

Beautiful weeks of summer followed, during which Martin could, on one side, have childlike good times. But inwardly there was seething unrest. He dreamed of dangerous cable car journeys which led him over deep valleys, feelings of panic . . . and: 'My parents don't hear me!' The following night came a dream with his father: a hurried car trip from an island onto solid ground . . . "I say to Papa that I am not going to come with him any more, because I don't feel safe with him." He was also separating himself inwardly from his brother, his close playmate: during a hard, violent fight Martin screamed at him, "I'll kill you!" and struck the glass door, which flew into shards. ". . . I am glad that the window broke," he wrote. "Just as the glass was shattered into a thousand pieces, so the hatred was destroyed toward my German and History teachers, toward my brother, toward this shitty society, toward everything and even toward some uncertain something. So I can also be angry, that feels tremendously good . . . Mama practically made me out to be a criminal. Phooey! I don't give a damn about anybody, about those who understand me and those who don't understand me. It felt really good. You're a lot freer . . ."
Freer for new transformative experiences, as I soon learned.

$$\diamond \; \diamond \; \diamond \; \diamond \; \diamond \; \diamond \; \diamond \; \diamond \; \diamond \; \diamond \; \diamond$$

Encounter With Death

A neighbor died. Martin was deeply affected. ". . . the person is dead. She isn't here on earth any more. The universe swallowed her up. We go back into nothingness. HORRIBLE! . . . The atmosphere of death is the most frightening of all feelings. An elemental force appears. You're just thrown off track." Then Martin remembered a nightmare, in which his parents were involved in a huge fight and killed themselves at the end. The question of death occupied Martin more and more often from this time on. His father had abdicated his overvalued, nearly god-like position; the elevated father image he had looked up to from far below had died. And too, the mother of yesterday was no longer there, since he had torn himself radically away from her. On whom could he now rely? "Who is God? What is a minute human being in this immense world?" He came one day to his therapy hour with this painful, ever more urgent question. I also felt powerless before it. Since I had already experienced in him that the answer was hidden in his own inner self and waited to be heard, I asked him to portray his difficult feelings in a drawing, and to wait to see what this 'oracle' communicated. The following picture was the result.

A conversation followed when the picture was finished, and he summarized his thoughts in a description of it:

> "The water flows and sweeps everything along with it. It never comes to a stop, but is constantly swept along by time. It comes out of the dark and goes into the dark, like life. The water means life, for plants and animals. The stream . . . sweeps everything with it, plunges into great depths and dangers, and yet it comes back out again and flows toward new adventures. No one knows where it comes from, no one knows where it goes. The water . . . disappears and later appears, beginning again at the beginning. In the moment of the picture it is simply there. It is in the middle of the picture. The center: life, raging, turbulent, calming . . . I would like . . . to be the flowers . . . The grass and the flowers have a hard struggle for their existence . . . They manage it despite highs (periods of drought) and lows (rainstorms and

Figure 14 *The Waterfall (drawing)*

floods)... The cacti as a symbol of death ... at the edge of
time, of life, of death ... Their arms are lifted stiffly up to the
heavens, as if they are awaiting help. The sand ... Millions of
grains lie there loose, infinite, lost? Each grain of sand, however
small it may be, is a piece of infinity, of a puzzle, a view of
which is not granted to us men. If a piece is missing, the desert
is incomplete ... The sun ... light, warmth ... the form of a
ball. It will not be taken from its course ... beyond the border of
life and death. The water and the sun are ... completely opposite ..., only something in common: they both save life ... The
three primal elements, water, air (desert wind) and the barren
earth are united in this picture."

The picture and Martin's thoughts about it instilled in us an
amazing calm in face of the reflections about life and death which
had made us so speechless at the beginning. Astonishing and
moving, how Martin described his place in the great All! The individual and the infinite balance each other. The individual is an
integral part of the whole; the All, in turn, gives the individual a
reliable and eternal frame. These communications from deep
within him required no further analysis or interpretation. I was
grateful that in my shaken state a poem, which Goethe wrote on a
Swiss journey, in front of a waterfall in Lauterbrunnental, occurred to me as a spontaneous amplification.

Song of the Spirits over the Waters
(Johann Wolfgang von Goethe)

Man's soul
Is like water:
From Heaven it comes,
To Heaven it rises,
And down again
To Earth it must return,
Forever alternating . . .

Soul of Man,
How like water you are!
Fate of Man,
How like wind you are!

Opposites

Half a year had now passed since Martin had fallen into his darkest crisis. A great deal had changed in and around him. Now his world collapsed again, as he experienced it. Again doubts about the meaning of life weighed heavily upon him. He felt indescribable sadness, mixed with rage and fear: he could not breathe and his heart stood still; he was tortured by thoughts of death. "The climax of my depression has been reached ..." Such were his words in his diary. In our hours he sat wordlessly at the sandtray.

When Martin could give his agitation visible shape in this sandplay, his inner "waves" calmed down noticeably; he came to himself and to a perceptible peace. Here is his description of the sandplay:

Figure 15 *Raging Sea (sandplay, detail)*

"A tiny rowboat tossed in the wildly raging sea. The little oarsman is nearly overwhelmed by the great load he is carrying,. Two big fish are approaching, one black and one white; one

wants to eat the oarsman and his boat, the other wants to help
him. In the background we see (not in the illustration) the
'Black Death' on a steed; then, in a raised position, Poseidon,
the god of the sea; and still further back, on a cliff, a city with a
lighthouse. In the other corner wagons and men are sinking in
the tide."

In this sandplay, the resumption of an earlier process is plain.
During the conversation which followed, several elements
seemed very familiar to us: the oppressive burden, the meeting of
the opposites, the threat of sinking and death. With a look back at
previous pictures he also quickly remembered the healing associations. In this way he could go back to earlier pictures and symbols more and more quickly and successfully, also in later "relapses" or "after-pains." What appeared to me to be new in this
last sandplay was the search for a balance between the powers,
which in a synthesis suggested a wholeness: the black fish and the
white fish; the 'Black Death' and the sea god; the going under and
the overcoming. Here death no longer has the absoluteness of 'all
or nothing'; it no longer endangers the whole person. Rather the
dying is balanced with a new confidence. The thought occurred to
us that some things in his life really must come to an end (childhood ideals, exaggerated goals, hopes needing to be abandoned),
so that another, greater strength could be realized.

The meeting of opposites and their effect on each other became become a *leitmotif* in Martin's pictures and sandplays. At
one time narrow city life and the freedom of nature stood in opposition, at another time monotonous civilization and contented
individualism, and at another fear of authority and the destructive fury, Good and Evil. White sheep, from which, however, "the
white color is crumbling," highways and flowers, which grow out
of the cracks in the cement, a white helpful and a black devouring
whale, a bleak black life, a beautiful and ideal hereafter, "war between suns and moons"—more and more the initially incompati-
ble opposites came into relationship with each other. Separated at
the beginning from each other by mountains and walls (in the
sandplay), little by little they became connected by links such as
tunnels and rivers.

Here is Martin's short description (slightly expanded by me) of
his sandplay 'Opposites':

"Two entirely different areas are separated from each other by a
thick fence. A deep tunnel leads across from here (right). Over
there it is prettier, more natural, more decent. By comparison

Figure 16 *Opposites (Sandplay)*

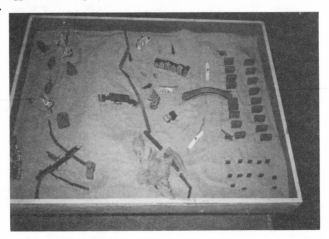

here on the right is a dismal city, but close by, connected by a
bridge, is a peaceful village. A river flows through the tunnel
over to the other side. The ships struggle against the current and
sail upstream."

Martin's diary entries seem to me to be an important supple-
ment to, and extension of, his sandplay:

"I had a talk with Mother about death . . . I believe in a full and
complete life hereafter, for the soul of a man can never be destroyed. But I get incredibly uneasy with such thoughts. I become afraid . . ., dizziness and half-hallucinations, I mean, I
have the feeling that I hear voices, and I don't feel as if I'm really myself and here at this moment any more. (Temporal and
spatial boundary disintegration!) . . . before going to sleep had
to think over and over again about the subject of death . . . in a
dream fell suddenly into a black hole . . ., thought I had to die
. . ., fear, abyss, fright . . . Falling asleep is like dying."

This sandplay gave his gloomy, heavy thoughts and feelings another dimension. It permitted a subtly differentiated way of looking at things and supported a further development. Here, two
irreconcilable worlds confront each other. They are clearly separated from one another by a fence. But there are attempts to overcome the opposites: a steamroller is working its way forward
against the mountain which divides the two worlds. And inside
the right area, in which rectangular, uncomfortable proportions

dominate, we see a peaceful village, linked with the regimented city by a bridge. And finally, the separated sides are connected underground by a tunnel, through which a river flows from right to left. The ships "put up a fight" against this direction of flow, as if to say, "We don't want to give in to the natural current, to let ourselves be carried into the dark, the unknown.' But what energy it takes to swim against the stream, to hold onto the clear, conscious and controllable world! We understand Martin's fear of falling asleep: sleep leads ever closer to the dark and unconscious, just like a natural 'river'. The fear means, therefore, fear of the contents of his unconscious. He hints in his diary that behind this lurks even the danger of going mad, that is—without that safe grounding in visible reality—to be swallowed up by the unconscious. Falling asleep also arouses in him thoughts of death. How meaningful it is that in their mythology the ancient Greeks regarded the god of sleep, Hypnos, as the brother of the god of death, Thanatos.

Martin's striving for a firm footing in everyday reality seemed to me to be highly legitimate, when I considered what deep abysses opened up in his dreams and fantasies. Indeed, perhaps our therapy, which can be compared with a descent into the depths of his own soul, required a correspondingly heavy counterweight in his home and school activities. I was pleased that cycling and playing tennis with his friend were occasionally more important than his dreambook and diary. For this same reason the frequency of therapy with a young person should be in the correct 'dosage'. With too infrequent hours the trust, in the doctor and in his own soul, which is necessary to dare the encounter with the inner dark and mysterious aspects, cannot develop. On the other hand, with too frequent hours the equally important occupation with the outer world and the support found in everyday life, so important as a protective counterbalance, could be neglected.

The question of the opposites intensified further. The outer cause was a huge marital battle between his parents, which triggered such fears of death that he again had to look for sanctuary in his parent's bed—just in the greatest 'trouble spot'! He tried to retreat into security. But at the same time a new, ruthless opposition to, even a reckoning with, his parents stirred in him. He now painfully remembered how, when his mother had years ago been in the throes of a crisis, he had experienced her as being as helpless as a child, and how he had had to carry more responsibility than he could. At that time he had looked to his father for support, but felt something like a wall between them. For years his father has treated him too much like an adult, because for a long time Martin has not felt as adult inside as he appeared to the outside. Now he saw these things more clearly and felt an indescribable rage. "I won't play your game any more!" he could say to his parents' faces. Moreover he intended to write "another whole book" about these experiences, so that it "comes out". It is like vomiting; when it is out, one feels freer. At this time Martin's father, at mid-life,was in the throes of a deep crisis, and needed ambulatory, then later even in-patient, psychiatric treatment. The father-image had 'cracked' once more, and lost more of its dependability.

Search For God

With these reflections Martin soon began to think about his image of God, which had now also been severely shaken. His father had stamped the image of a vengeful God into him. Now he was looking for a new God. The image of God must develop outward from deep within, he believes, but he is missing these personal depths. He felt as if he were suspended, in an airless room, between his shattered trust in his father and an inaccessible God. As an example from his own depths I received the following

Dream
"I am driving with my father in a little wagon; it is like a
roller coaster. Papa points out the tower on the mountain;
dark clouds hang over the peak. Papa stands up, the little
wagon rocks wildly and dangerously. Then to my great
distress Papa stands up again . . . I know that I am lost . . . I
am still clinging to the little wagon, which seems smaller and
smaller (only as big as my hand)—Ahh! I'm falling—Out—I
am lost—My heart stands still . . . Then I wake up."

His father's orientation in the heights, his pointing out of the tower on the peak, his risky and repeated standing up could all be indications of his one-sided lifestyle, with which he caused the greatest distress to himself and others. Both the danger and the senselessness of such a one-sided attitude are shown here in the dream.

Here is Martin's short description of his sandplay (next page):

Raised in the middle, on a solid foundation, stands a white castle, which makes him a bit afraid; it has to do also with religion. On one side, the left, is a lovely land with a river, bridge and pretty houses. On the right two steam shovels and a tank push against the mountain with all their might, as if they wanted to level it. Houses and trees are toppling in the chaos. The three men are parts of his [Martin's] personality. The one farthest to the left is shooting a cannon against the shoving superior strength on the right (the excavators and tank). The second,

Figure 17 *The White Church (Sandplay)*

near the big tree, is succumbing to this strength. The third, behind the castle, is thinking about what to do. But he has no overview and no idea what is happening on that side of the wall, on
the right. But in any case the castle stands firm there; nothing
will harm it. The white color of the castle represents the Good.
Only later does the castle seem to us to be a church.

The stark opposites, up until now standing rigidly and motion-
lessly against one another, come now into motion, indeed, even
go after one another. On one side revolutionary powers are at
work; the entire landscape threatens to change. On the other side
is Martin's ego, represented by three various men. It reacts on
three different levels. On one, it vehemently opposes the changes;
on another, faced with the superior strength it lets them happen,
but threatens to perish with them. Thirdly it contemplates, that
is, tries to grasp the meaning of the developments, in order best to
do justice to them. Amidst these confusing events the mountain
in the middle appears to be essential: it is the only reliable point
of reference

Our conversation brought us around to consideration of our
relationship and the help which Martin expected from me. I
heard that I should be like this solid mountain for him, firmly
rooted in the ground and at the same time conveying an "upward" orientation. It has something to do with God and also
makes him a little afraid, he says of this mountain. His experience

of God was being differentiated: he saw not only the 'beloved God' of childhood, and not only the vengeful Father-God. The Divine was offering a middle ground, a central orientation, yet was at the same time unfathomable and therefore frightening. Events, the inner and outer developmental processes, now circled around this center. But it is equally his own center: this depiction in the sandplay was produced by *his* hand and from his own fantasy! It is the first clear portrayal of his Self, that imaginary psychic regulatory center of the maturing personality.

To the degree that the poles had an effect on each other, it was less and less clear to Martin which side was 'good' and which 'bad'. The clear, childish moral system was no longer right. The 'beautiful, ideal world' in his sandplays became unreal, even kitschy to him. In any case, it no longer represented the entire truth for him. At the same time he experienced the aggressive, destructive elements—likewise in the sandplay—in a completely new light. He could no longer hold these in such contempt. Rather, it was also refreshing to him to show, and live, this side, because it too belongs to him. When he spoke this way, I felt a "real man" in front of me. Indeed, he was now closer to his wholeness, had brought a piece of his shadow up from out of the dungeon of the unconscious and assimilated it into consciousness.

In our work the question sometimes arose: Does it require a therapy, a specialist, for these developments? Would these developments not have happened entirely by themselves, without outside intervention? Or in other words: Are the creative communications in the therapy an expression of what has already been achieved, or do they really give the healing impulse for the growth toward wholeness? The appropriate answer is probably: Both! What is suggested in symbolic play as well as in dreams and other communications is already reality, at least in embryonic form. But making it visible leads above and beyond that embryonic suggestion to a possibility of experience, which affords its coming into consciousness. A dialogue between the creative soul and the ego-consciousness results, as I have described it above with the example of sandplay.

As patient as well as therapist one gains in this work a deep respect for the reality of the psyche, for the objectivity of the unconscious. This attitude contributes to the fruitful realization of these psychic powers, and it protects us from the egocentric question: Is it thanks to me that this healing was possible, or is this healing completely independent of me; has it even come into being in defiance of my efforts? This process can be beautifully compared to the course of events of a birth. As obstetrician we have the duty to preserve the existing life and escort it out through a narrow passage into the light of day. The new life, which we place in the arms of the woman who bore it, is not our work. At best we have contributed to it, so that it didn't suffocate or otherwise suffer damage. We can experience the increasing coming of consciousness as a 'Birth of the Self'.

Symbol of the Self

The year came to a close. Martin took this as the occasion to look back: the year was as full of events and changes as many previous years taken together. Our relationship underwent a change: Martin was suddenly relying on me less. He seemed to go his own way more, without confiding all his thoughts and feelings in me. Only much later did I hear from him that during this period he very much admired a young woman, who greatly occupied his thoughts and feelings. He was striving to distance himself from me and from his parents, probably in order to be better able to recognize his own path; that became clear to me later. In an essay about his father, and another about his mother—both written a year after the great crisis—he describes the increasingly clear space which he has won from his parents.

A short time later he gave me, at my suggestion, another family portrait, again with everyone 'transformed' into animals.

More graphically than words ever could, the drawing makes apparent where he stands, and where the other members of the family stand in relationship to him. All have 'forsaken' the water and are now on and above the earth floor. At the top is Martin himself, sitting on a branch as a bird of prey. He can now, he says, fly away at any time, whenever it pleases him, but can also come home to his family, if it becomes too much for him later. His brother, as a giraffe, can already look a little bit toward the horizon, too. The mother, as a kangaroo, is directly under Martin, but with her gaze turned more toward the father, a rhinoceros. Here the objective development of the rest of the family interests us less than what these portrayals subjectively mean to Martin. Thus: what has happened with his image of the mother in him, his image of the father in him?

A kangaroo mother offers a pocket for the warm security of her child. The bird sits on the branch exactly over this kangaroo, and is also related to it in color, but otherwise is probably hardly interested any longer in slipping into that warm pocket. Regression, thus, has more the value of a reminiscence—wonderful, when it

101

Figure 18 *Family as Animals II (Drawing)*

is still possible in memory to snuggle up safe with mother! Certainly this mother is no longer all-devouring as she was at one time in the sea (see Figure 9). The father no longer stands over, but instead under him! Instead of being threatening to Martin, he has now retreated into his own armor; as Martin would say, "He can struggle by himself with his problems, I am now free!"

Also in sandplay (Figure 19) Martin gave me an example of his search for his own, personal life path. Like the family portrait, this sandplay also takes up an earlier, similar motif, that of the journey through the desert that he had made a year before. What has happened in this year?

For the moment, here is our joint description of his sandplay:

> A clearly-marked path leads the man with his pack donkey to a well-ordered, square village, which is surrounded by a fence. One can feel at home there, the world is orderly. Then a bridge leads over a river. The path further on is blocked by a sort of labyrinth, at the beginning of which lie a black and a white die with the number 3 and 5. Behind this is a city, which is built on the impression of Martin's right hand, which he had pressed into the sand. There are no men there; only a well in the middle. In the well swims a duck, who shows the traveller the right direction. The path goes on further through a sort of moonscape to a house in the corner. That is the goal. In the river are three fish, perhaps salmon. They find their way upstream. Here, too, a duck points in the right direction, to the place where they were

Figure 19 *The Second Journey*

born. There stands a triangular temple, whose function is to
contain the entire world in this sandplay. The triangularity of
the temple, which stands raised on the hill, reminds Martin of
the three elements: fire, earth, water (Martin doesn't mention
the air as an additional element!).

One year later—and what a change! First the clarity of the or-
ganization impressed me. Four places are linked by two crossing
diagonals. The whole forms a harmonious square. Four aspects of
his personality are addressed here and placed into relationship
with one another by the path. The family, which in Figure 13 was
left behind crying, is missing here; he appears to have gotten over
it. The donkey as the carrier of the burden calls to mind the patience and the effort which are necessary for this journey. It,
along with the 'oxen' (both in Figure 13 and in Feng's story) reminds us of the important animals in the stall at Bethlehem. And
the donkey is seldom missing in depictions of the flight of the
holy family to Egypt. The ass, with its stubborn, stupid way, is the
carrier of the dark aspects of human nature. It is fortunate that
Martin has found a carrier for these, as well. But however difficult
the path may be, in this sandplay it is at least clearly marked by
the black stones. The somewhat mechanically-designed first village with its confining fence is also reminiscent of earlier
sandplays (Figure 16). There Martin—with somewhat one-sided
contempt—sets the rigidity of the city against another, more liv-

ing (opposite) principle. Here the simple, linear order is an important, integrative component of the whole. Without this preliminary step there is no going on.

In the center stands the bridge, as the central symbol for the entire sandplay: Opposites are being linked, bridged into a whole. Again an ordeal must be undergone. A puzzle or oracle must be understood and followed. The two dice are opposites, black and white. The secret seems to be to perceive the opposites as an integral whole, whereupon the further path through the labyrinth opens up to the wayfarer. The symbolism of '3' and '5' was at first mysterious to us.

The next stage is of great meaning: his own city. His own, for the foundation was formed by Martin's own right hand. I tried to understand this firm resolution: Here I press my hand into the sand, that is my land, here I build my city! This gave me an impression of the strength of his inner personality as well as his confidence to build his life here on this earth. The image of the city confines the other residents; Martin is integrating himself into a collective, he belongs to it. In the middle of the city stands the well, with which we are acquainted from the other sandplay as the Fount of Wisdom. The well is also a refreshing symbol of life, which gets its power from out of the depths (of the unconscious).

Until now, only a part of Martin's growing toward wholeness was visible. The path will go on. Thanks to the sign of the infallible duck the wanderer leaves the now trusted ground of the city and ventures into a completely foreign realm, which looks as if it were on the Moon. I had to think of a sleepwalker, who—harkening to the mad whims of the Moon—pursues a goal which is totally unknown to his waking consciousness. Is it perhaps his inner moods which whisper the correct way to him, even perhaps a certain madness? Why indeed do we call madmen 'lunatics', those influenced by the Moon? Why indeed do 'children and fools' impress us secretly, despite the fact that we outwardly laugh at them? I had a sense of this in conversations with the mentally ill in clinics: they are not of this world, in which our senses are trapped. Their minds are freely open to the unknown in them, indeed they are overwhelmed by it. Therefore I never had the desire to become a 'lunatic', but all the same a great respect for these 'crazy people' arose within me; it was as if their pioneering journey were on our behalf, on behalf of the 'normal ones', who do not leave the ground they know.

Now, at least in the framework of the sand-tray and under the protection of our therapeutic bond, Martin ventured off on his trip along the lonely path into the unknown. He reached his "destination", as he himself called it: his individual house. It stands there isolated, it has 'individuated' in the truest sense of the word, found its independent autonomy. In the Analytical Psychology of C. G. Jung, 'Individuation' is the fulfilling rounding-out of the personality, the unfolding of the qualities contained in the 'Self', the dark as well as the light. With Martin there was not yet a question of a well-rounded personality, but— again in the safety of therapy—he dared, so to speak, a 'test of wholeness'.

Truly his goal was thereby reached. Yet somehow the path goes on, in a spiritual, transcendent sense, as will be shown. Three fish now point out the way. We reflected on the astonishing feature of salmon, who in the course of their life-cycle find their way back from the sea to the waters of their birth. Through this expansion of our reflections, which in Jungian Psychology we call an amplification, Martin's 'world-view' was connected to a larger realm of ideas: the fish is also a symbol of early Christianity. The fish is Christ, He Who was baptised in water. The letters of the Greek word ICHTHYS (= fish) are at the same time the first letters of Iesous—Christos—Theou—hYos—Soter (Jesus—Christ—God's—Son—Saviour) and therefore the central ideas of Christian sacred teaching. The number three calls to mind the Trinity: Father, Son, Holy Ghost; just as does the triangular temple, which the three fish find at the spring of their origin. For Martin it is also, as we know from the earlier sandplay, the Fount of Wisdom. He has not quite attained it, when he speaks of the three elements; earth, water, fire. Where is the air, the element of the spiritual?

I was relieved that this young man didn't yet show much personal completeness; I sensed a danger that he neglected the tasks, appropriate to his age, which life had set him. The overall arrangement in his sandpicture, all the same, hinted at such completeness. The four regions (collectively handed-down order, personal order, finding of himself, spiritual way) are bound by two diagonals into a whole. In the middle, where the paths cross, stands the bridge, as a symbol of the union of opposites. It could here correspond to the fifth element of the alchemists, the *Quinta Essentia*. In a mysterious way the question, "three or five?" is indeed already indicated at the entrance to the labyrinth. Typically, an oracle's meaning is often made clear only in retrospect, and this is true here, too: not three but rather five elements mean wholeness. Martin knows this in his depths, as the sandplay reveals. But the conscious access to this knowledge is yet lacking. His knowledge of the three also corresponds much more easily to his age, insofar as three is the number of the dynamic processes, a resolute 'Yes' to active masculine development.

◇ ◇ ◇ ◇ ◇ ◇ ◇ ◇ ◇ ◇ ◇

Back Into Life

The rhythm of our therapy hours relaxed. Daily life demanded its dues. Over the summer vacation Martin worked on the assembly line in a chocolate factory, more because his parents wanted him to experience the harsh world of work than out of his own initiative. He became aware that he all too often sacrificed himself in order to please his parents. Increasingly he experienced conflict within himself. He felt a desire to break violently out of the mold into which he felt he was pressed. He would have preferred to shock the adults with crazy haircuts and clothing, but outwardly he behaved more and more pronouncedly 'normal'. In the church community he organized round-table discussions among young people. It is true that this was in keeping with his thoughtful, introverted nature, but he sensed that there was yet another nature living in him, to which he paid insufficient attention.

Between these two natures he lived in a conflict of loyalty. At least in his quiet little room, in his diary, the other side broke through uninhibitedly. His thoughts at times sounded like those of a determined terrorist: unspeakable rage against the inhumanity of this world, against the devastating war machinery of the superpowers, against crimes against life and the environment. I felt obliged to warn him against translating his wild plans into fact and thus becoming himself a destroyer of life and environment, when he proclaimed, for example: "I am now a volcano. All the filthy little men around me can perish in the lava stream of destruction which pours out of me! . . . Destroys laws! Breaks limits! Anarchy, chaos, death! . . "

These outbreaks were not new, but his wide-awake interest in and feeling of responsibility for the environment were new. Also new was his capacity to regard the evil world, which he condemned, as an essential part of him, which also wanted to live, but which until now had threatened to suffocate under outward good behavior and conformity. At that time his face expressed a maturing, distinct personality. He had also outwardly developed his own personal image.

During his father's deepest depressive crisis and in-patient clinic stay, Martin also had to take over the responsible role of an adult in the family. But now, in contrast to earlier times, he could carry and bear the responsibility. He now behaved like a father toward his brother. With dismay he saw that his brother was in the same trouble that he himself had been in a short time ago. I gave his parents the name of one of my colleagues, so that the brother, too, could get help. I myself was not suitable; I would have put myself into a complicated conflict of loyalty between the two brothers.

This was the background against which he produced his last sandplay (Figure 20). His description was something like this:

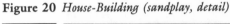

Figure 20 *House-Building (sandplay, detail)*

"Behind there they are building a highway and filling up part of the pond in preparation for it. The fish must retreat into the rest of the pond. On the right is a garbage dump with a steam shovel. The woods are lovely, but there, too, some trees will be felled. Things will be destroyed, but something new will come from it. In the middle a house is being built; one can see the foundation already. The builder of the house is proud of this monument, so he lets someone photograph him."

'The world is not pleasant. But it just *is* that way, so let's make the best of it!' Thus we could summarize the central idea of this sandplay. Martin was a very conscious witness to the abuse and displacement of Nature by man and his technology. But are these processes not also graphic images of what Martin experienced inwardly? His parents' disputes made a mockery of their pretty ideas of peace. He saw himself confronted everywhere with conflicting demands. Where did he himself stand? Only a small space is left to him for the unfolding of his previously boundless-seeming powers. Adaptation, limitation, and sacrifice are necessary everywhere.

A meeting and balancing between nature and culture is also taking place within him. His inexpressible sexual stirrings do not fit at all with his ideal of love. Undertaking the responsibility of being an adult means forfeiting childish freedom. Achieving knowledge and consciousness of the world means increasing distance from a purely natural and instinctive understanding of the world. And so he is gripped by inner conflicting demands as well. It is necessary to find a passable way somewhere between them. Facing the gain is a loss, which is painful to take. Martin appears prepared for the loss; he can now live with it. Would he otherwise decide to build his house in the middle of these contradictory happenings? He documents the fact that he stands by this, even thinks this act a historical one, with the photographic record, which will preserve the memorable moment for posterity.

This picture marked the end of our work, which, looking back, was a journey through a great darkness. Now everyday life demanded its due.

A few years later I had the opportunity to look at this moment again with Martin, with the calm and composure of retrospection, and to ask what he was able to build on this foundation.

Martin had grown into a self-confident young man, with an impressively clear countenance. He knew what he wanted, and he made it plain to me with composure rather than in a tough way. I steered our conversation to the stressful months following his confirmation. It is worth noting that he seems to have forgotten this time. It made me think of the enchantment of an 'underworld', through which he had travelled in my company, but from which he was now separated by the river of 'forgetfulness'. He himself was amazed at how the feelings of that time had slipped from him. We remembered his picture of the tunnel. What he had experienced there now lay far behind and in the darkness. Naturally, forgotten does not mean lost. Rather, the difficult experiences of this time were changed in him, as if he had not just forgotten, but 'digested' and incorporated them. It was a dreadful time, he remembered anyway, but important and perhaps right for him. The thought also came to him that it had been like a birth. And who can remember the details of his own birth? In the desperation of the confinement and fear of this process of transition, he had relied on help and being accompanied.

He had easily finished school and graduated. He submitted to his bitter military service without giving in to the temptation to get himself out of it with the help of 'his' psychiatrist. He revolted strongly against the shrill military drills and the subjugation of his weaker and more cautious fellows, to whom he felt a fraternal connection, but he did this more inwardly than outwardly. Not that he had swallowed his anger. He sought out men of like mind, to whom he spoke frankly. At home in his village he went to the Catholic church, to which his mother had re-converted, to have discussions with young people. He wanted to communicate something to them which he had missed in his own church. With young women he had only shy, sporadic contact. For a few months, he told me later, he had had a girlfriend, but it turned out that their views were too different.

More out of duty than desire he began studying at the university: history. He simply had to study some field for his intended profession of teaching. A hidden motive for studying history could be his old interest in getting to the bottom of things, to learn why it all turned out the way it did, within himself as well as in the world outside.

But the deeper his thoughts and questions penetrated, the less his studies satisfied him. It seemed, he told me, completely obvious and natural that he had now decided to study theology. In the church he can give young people that which he himself received during adolescence.

Reflections on the Stories of Maria and Martin

This book is the result of a pressing concern, and not simply the wish to expose the exciting processes of development of two young people to curious readers. To the contrary: this sharing required painful surrender, by myself as well as by Martin and Maria. These two people began to understand the universal meaning of their stories for a larger circle of similarly, and also differently, afflicted people of every age. And they were therefore prepared—with their names changed, of course—to make their innermost experience public.

Maria and Martin were patients who needed psychiatric, that is, medical-psychological care. Entirely normal, everyday adolescents would also have been suited to give us insight into the basic patterns of this important transitional phase in human life. Two reasons spoke on behalf of my choice of these patients.

First of all, the needs of these two people led me to become unusually deeply absorbed in their thoughts and feelings. It was also because of their neediness that they were really ready for this path into the depths. I could not have received this sort of rich material about unconscious events, which grew out of the regular, trusting dialogue in medical therapy, from a 'normal' young person. I am convinced that every young person holds a similar richness within, but one which only rarely shows itself in this way, and then only subtly

Second, the stories of these 'sick' people are suited to demonstrate the underlying transition process especially clearly. For it seems to me that the ill, who dare to immerse themselves in their painful experiences, live out the pattern of transformation as if through a magnifying glass. It was amazing to me that both of them, Maria and Martin, (at least apparently) lost this magnified view again after the darkest and most difficult time. Only a faint, astonished idea was there, when I spoke with them later about their past dreams and inner images. The 'magnifying glass' had served its purpose in the transformation of the personality and was now no longer necessary.

The weakening of the sense of reality during this period of radical change, which I described by way of introduction, must not continue. After this time it is part of the task of adolescents to obtain and preserve a clear, conscious view of the outer demands of life. The time of fairy tales and dreams is past; the serious business of life begins. Yet on the other hand we know the eternal youths who are caught in this land of dreams and fairy tales, be it because they cannot withstand a certain seductive undertow, or be it because they accomplished the journey through the personal and collective depths only incompletely, and must now make it up again and again.

My concern, which forms the basis for this book, arises from a concern of this young woman and young man, which was not expressed during the period of our therapeutic companionship, but which was clear to me. Martin expressed it later: in his profession he would like to give the young people today what he himself experienced at that time: encouragement and support in the gloomiest and most hopeless period of crisis. With his younger brother he could only stand by aghast and dismayed. Now he has the maturity and the professional qualifications to help other young people.

Puberty involves all of us, the entire community. This is to say that the puberty crisis of individual adolescents, just like the crisis of youth in general, 'wants' to communicate to the collective something of the dynamics of the deep unconscious, which find their expression in dreams and fantasies, but also in the 'impossible' behavior of teenagers. There is a natural power of renewal in young people. Adolescents who cannot approach their parents with their concerns are prone to emergency solutions, as I portrayed them above with Maria and Martin.

Youth as a collective chooses such ways, if society answers youth unrest only with measures to preserve 'order', instead of using the energies being freed for a new, broader orientation of the society.

The young person of today—this is supposed to be scientifically proven—has no specific problems which can be described as the need of our youth. Is this really true? I am convinced that today's young people have learned 'not to have problems,' because they seem to stand in the way of the currently fashionable developments and adaptations, I am eager to see, not without some apprehension, what from the denied dynamics of youth will later emerge or break out, having been put off for perhaps an entire generation. We know the rhythmic change of peace and chaos, of extraversion and introversion in the young. The duration of the phases of this rhythm seems to be, curiously enough, about twelve years, which corresponds to the life span of an (albeit early-maturing) child up to the beginning of puberty, therefore a child-generation. I would like to call to mind the following years of unrest:

—about 1908: youth agitation;

—1920: the confused, crazy "Twenties" begin;

—1932/33: the culmination of unrest, leading to the outbreak of the "Thousand-year Reich";

—1944/45: Collapse of the "Reich";

—1956: Revolt in Hungary and corresponding sympathetic movements in the West;

—1968: Revolt in Czechoslovakia, the " '68 Prague Spring";

—1980: Youth unrest in many major cities (in Europe)

—1992: ?

This list came to me out of an entirely subjective, and, I must say, 'autosuggestive' reflection. It would be interesting and important to review such uncertain rhythms objectively and critically in a disciplined general study.

Yes, the young person of today is problem-free—so long as one leaves out of consideration those who in the current latent phase (in the rhythm assumed) would be happily considered by society as not belonging to it: the drug addicts, criminals, suicides and psychotics. Society might also like to excuse this simplified, striking list. But this list should indicate that today, in the years of the seemingly, but only outwardly, peaceful youth, the energies of renewal are captured and conserved in narrowly-circumscribed areas or are completely lost, to remain with the aforementioned fringe groups: in the drug treatment centers, prisons, graveyards and psychiatric clinics.

At least in my professional setting, psychiatry, it is becoming vividly clear to me what value is revealed among the sick, that is to say, in the adolescents who, as far as a feeling of "health" goes, are seen as no longer acceptable or no longer normal, be they depressive, addicted or psychotic. If we can succeed in considering these sick individuals as the 'magnifying glass' for pressing youth questions, we can see them as pioneers of youth rather than as marginal failures. In my work with Martin and Maria it was of central importance that they learn of this special value. The idea that their suffering was not only for themselves, but could also be of meaning for others, gave them a particular lift. In retrospect it was just their crises in the adolescent years which gave them a meaning for the further shaping of their lives.

The stories of Maria and Martin also gave me courage to walk across a good many 'bridges,' when the abysses seemed so very threatening, the obstacles again so insurmountable. For my work with other adolescents in emergencies they gave me pictures, which today serve me as 'bridges' over hopeless-seeming situations. They are images of trust, of trust in oneself, of trust in fundamental powers which come from out of the personal depths, and finally of trust in a greater order, which stretches beyond the personal.

We are touching here upon areas which really go far beyond the tools and the task of our profession. Through encounters with modern young people the professional image and commission of a psychologist is changing: with respect to adolescents I feel myself to be a caretaker of the soul or a medicine man, quite similar to the way in which the primitives describe him. So with Martin, when the course of suffering and healing took on the character of a confirmation, or better, of an initiation rite. And I had, and have, the duty to stand faithfully by during this act.

The encounter with the unconscious and particularly with the powers of the collective unconscious brings about in many such a far-reaching change that it is as if a divine revelation occurs to them. He who finds his Self is touched by the divine, and a supportive and comforting connectedness to a heavenly and timeless order is never entirely lost. I do not dare say more here, in order to make clear that our healing work has pastoral characteristics, without our intending it.

Dear readers, finally and in conclusion I would like to come to you personally. Many of you are fathers and mothers of adolescents in puberty, others are rattled and shaken in your own ways like adolescents.

Mothers and fathers can be painfully pushed into their own search for themselves in going through the crisis with their growing children. Biographically these parents are more or less at their own mid-life, at the 'zenith' of their life, where the curve begins to slope downwards. This is for them occasion to reflect upon the deeper meaning of their existence and to go more consciously on the path to their own self-development.

Martin and Maria's journeys at adolescence may also in some ways be like yours. Many of you will perhaps find that you have experienced similar loneliness, fear and hopelessness, and can test for yourselves the means they took to find a way out of their difficulties. The more deeply the hopelessness is felt, the more intense can be the experiences which lead to paths crossing the bridge to new shores.

The images which appear to young people in puberty and adolescence, just in their own deep despair, are of archetypal meaning, that is to say, they are collective primordial images, in which all men and women participate, beyond the bounds of time and of peoples. These images can encourage the acceptance of even a person's darkest experiences, such as grief, rage, depression or illness, as important stages of a path to maturity. Indeed, they give that person a life-meaning, which helps prepare him to go over this 'dark abyss'.

I would like to thank Maria and Martin, as well as many other young people, with all my heart, for giving us this view of the precious and helpful image-realm of the soul, and for showing us the way over the bridge.

Further Reflections on Childhood, Adolescence, and Death

◇ ◇ ◇ ◇ ◇ ◇ ◇ ◇ ◇ ◇ ◇

Children Change Parents*

In the light of the generally heard conviction that almost anything is feasible by means of education, I am sure you will agree that the title for this paper is not just bold, but also refreshing, since the tables are turned, and we, the adult educators, are those who are pinpointed and to whom things are being done. When the title was put to me by the organizers of an international forum, it induced me to rethink a lot of fundamental issues, to look for new perspectives in my role as a child psychiatrist and therapist, as well as in that of a family father.

What I am going to say is intended more for the fathers and mothers with whom I share the joys and suffering of parenthood than for a professional audience. The experiences and realizations I intend to discuss may affect many of you. Like myself, you are probably asking yourselves, 'Did I do the right thing? Did I live up to my duties as a parent?', and, just like me you will, I hope, come to the conclusion that you are not perfect parents. I rather like what Michael Rothman said when he pointed out that there are no ideal parents: 'Reasonably good' is probably the best we can hope for.

To describe the transformations which parents undergo in the course of becoming, or being, parents, I shall try to outline a collective history of development by analogy with the history of child development as it is taught to psychologists.

Parental development may actually start in childhood, while playing at 'fathers and mothers', a game where all the attention is focussed on the play baby. An inborn pattern of mothering or fathering is activated and practiced in this game which, in turn, has a transformative impact on the playing child. This illustrates the great importance of projective play.

As is frequently the case in life at large, children are first begotten in the mind! In this context we might want to mention the works and creations which are so dear to the hearts of their au-

*A talk given over South German Radio, 1988.

119

thors that they experience them as their 'children'. They too are a mirror and have their impact on the development of the personality of the author.

When it comes to the physical act of *procreation*, however, men and women are affected in very different ways. 'To become a father is not difficult', as the saying goes. This statement does not apply in equal measure to women. We merely need to look at the bodily and other changes which become so manifest in the mother-to-be that we can hardly fail to notice them. For this reason, the father-to-be becomes involved in the nine months' preparatory period early on. It may deprive him of some of his comforts and the tenderness he is used to from his wife, but it also confers a new role and a new status on him. *Pregnancy* requires that both parents relax and concentrate on the newly growing life. By participating in the experience of embryonic shelteredness in their own body, as it were, parents also get a chance to 'hatch' some aspects of their own personality which may have remained immature.

One woman told me that she experienced herself and her unborn child as though the two of them were wrapped up in a kind of invisible protective cover. It seemed to her as if all the familiar and everyday nuisances and concerns seemed to bounce off this protective wrapping. Some women have trouble or are incapable of cherishing nature's 'gift' to them and fight tooth and nail against the process of oncoming motherhood. In other cases, they do not feel ready to give the child something they themselves may have missed or failed to experience. Others fear that they will lose some of their freedom. Fortunately, nature or the inborn pattern of maternal behavior ultimately reclaims its own and tends to take over. As an expression of its physical presence, the child's first movements are a very impressive experience for the mother inasmuch as they are the first indication of the presence of the new and separate being.

As a man, I can only surmise what a mother may experience during *childbirth*. Extreme pain is coupled with the feeling of immense happiness, no doubt. She both 'dies' and 'is born' at the same time. In addition to the physical pain, the act of parturition is probably the mother's first lesson in detachment. No doubt, the fact that the father is spared the pain experience during delivery and the act of parting from the child is largely responsible for the fundamental difference between the father's and the mother's positions henceforth.

However, I doubt that at the bottom of their hearts fathers are *mere* fathers and mothers *nothing but* mothers. There seems to be an inner counterpart as well: the father's motherliness and the mother's fatherliness, qualities which may have been neglected as a result of biological differences and social expectations which may or may not be merely accidental. Being a father myself, I have experienced the need to allow leeway for and relive the act of birth in my own imagination.

Anyone who has been witness to the indescribable mystery of birth, in particular as the child's parent, cannot remain indifferent to the transcendental component of the event. The innocence and virginality of the child is so endearing and fascinating for us because we experience it as 'holy'. The child is our savior, redeemer, because it is whole and intact. It is the epitome of the wholeness and perfection we are striving for throughout life without ever being able to attain it during our temporal existence.

Expressed in psychological terms: we would say at this deeply moving moment the newborn infant receives the projection of our inner child which longs to be born and come to life. Potentially, the birth of our child would also signify our own 'birth'. If, however, our own unfulfilled hopes for growth are projected on the infant, they become an alien element and burden for the child and will prevent it from developing its own individuality.

With the presence of the *first child*, an entirely new situation is constellated. The child is a new point of reference which changes the polarized axis of the couple into a triangle. The single existing axis of relationship yields a threesome. The interaction between these three points of reference is a very complex one. Many a couple are taken by surprise and experience the resulting demands placed upon them as excessive. Often there are partners who do not feel ready to make room for the new child or, possibly, to cease being the partner's 'child'. On the other hand, our children may also be in a position to help us retrieve our own childhood and to make up for certain stages on which we may have missed out.

Children are not a remedy for partnerships which may seem to be condemned to failure, although a child may provide a new content for a relationship, especially when it happens unexpectedly. The partners may get to know each other from entirely new points of view and suddenly reveal hitherto unexpected qualities to each other.

For their parents, children are the gateway to the world. This is particularly true of our times, in which so many small nuclear families suffer from urban loneliness. As parents of newborn infants, we are addressed by people who never took any notice of us before. Our children's playmates draw our attention to neighbors whom we may have known until then only from seeing their names on the mailbox. Through the children's kindergarten and school, new contacts are generated for the parents. Moreover, as parents we develop new concerns for the affairs of the world and take responsibility for the future of the environment. Many parents might never get in touch with what is going on in today's world, were it not for their children.

The birth of the first child moves parents into a different genealogical position, either up or down one rank, depending on your perspective. Or, using an image, we might say that parents are like the outer skin of a flower bud which gradually gives way to a more central, vital layer of growth. The realization of having to take a back seat and the frailty of our own existence crops up time and again as we witness the stages of our children's development. If the challenge is accepted, children may become an important factor in their parents' development. For the confrontation with this plays a vital part in the process of becoming oneself, of *individuation* and therefore of life.

The child is an expression of the absence of space and time, it is an 'Anfangs- und Endwesen' (a 'being of beginnings and endings', C. G. Jung). Children therefore induce us to bridge the time between what has been and what will be, enabling us to reach beyond the straightjacket of a one-sided relationship to the present only. Fleeting experiences such as a baby's smile or the delicate searching movement of a tiny hand have hit me like lightning. Such gestures have put a lot of seemingly important run-of-the-mill aspects into perspective, as for example: What is the argument with my colleague to me, considering the proud beam on my daughter's face when she practices her first steps? After all, what I witness here belongs to a much greater, that is divine, order of things in which I have the privilege of being imbedded. Moreover, the fatherly responsibility awakened by my children is a counterpoise which is not merely burdensome, but enriching, even in my profession. Now I am able to listen to mothers talking about the early experiences with their children in deep sympathy, compared to the painstaking questioning I had to proceed to before.

By analogy with the actual birth, each further step in the child's development confronts the parents with the need to allow the child to grow, walk, and talk. And each one of these steps involves the child's gradual detachment from the parents. The more devoted the parents' love for their children, the greater the pains of such 'after-birth'. In the process, many a father gets the opportunity to suffer the pain of parturition in his own soul. During this gradual detachment, parents have to engage in a continual process of rethinking, in order to achieve a new balance. They have to refurbish the space which used to be taken up by their beloved child with life of their own. The children's development is therefore a continuous challenge for the parents to live their own life.

Are our own children truly ours? In a way, yes, and in a way, no. Similarities between us and our children seem to indicate that we are at least partially made of the same stuff. Then again, a child may display characteristics which are so different from anything which is familiar to us that we cannot help wondering how this child came to be ours. Doubtlessly, our example tends to leave a strong imprint on our children. Then again, we are amazed at certain gifts and peculiarities which we would barely have been able to impart or instill in the child in such a short time. In *biological terms*, we are dealing here with hereditary factors; *psychologically* speaking, however, it is also the share all people have in those age-old human experiences which C. G. Jung called the '*collective unconscious*'. Some respect for this dimension might help us not to think that either the good qualities or the problems of our children are exclusively our own doing. This may allay many guilt feelings and dampen a lot of grandiose parental pride.

The fascinating wealth of ideas which comes to light in children's games seems to me to be one expression of this treasure of collective knowledge which is gradually covered over and forgotten in the process of growing up. Children can help their parents to gain access to this forgotten archaic knowledge. As a result, parents can revive their own inner child and retrieve the kind of openness and free development which they lost in schools and professions and because of adaptation. 'Thou shalt become like children' should be understood in these terms and not as a one-sided exaltation or imitation of childlike unconsciousness. To remain an eternal child would be to miss the point. It is a matter of nourishing the process of adult consciousness with the energies in the depth of the unconscious.

Looked at in this light, it is by no means evident who educates whom, who changes or transforms whom, the children the parents or the reverse. Giving and taking seem to come in waves, establishing a balance of flow between parents and their children. In addition to the conscious influence that is exerted mutually, children live in deep unconscious unity with their parents, in 'participation mystique' according to Levy-Brühl. Children have dreams reflecting their parents' problems. They may be true 'seismographs' for what is wrong and express tensions to the great amazement of their parents who swear that they never communicated any of their worries or marital conflicts.

For parents, their children's ability to show the unconscious or the *parents' unlived life* constitutes a great opportunity, enabling them to see themselves reflected in the child as in a mirror. It is a first step towards a transformation, in the course of which parents learn to accept themselves as they are, including their shadow, instead of putting all the blame on the child. This is a necessary process for the child's free development; otherwise it will be smothered under the weight of the parents' unconscious contents and their projection. And therefore it will be unable to become itself.

It seems to me that the child's relationship to the parent of the opposite sex, the son-mother or daughter-father relationship, is of special importance. Perhaps you'll join me in a reflection on the changes I feel were brought about in me as the father of a little girl who was just about one year old at the time of writing. My firstborn had been a son and, for me, the fact that he turned out to be a boy was nearly a matter of course: I had wished for him so much. After the birth of our daughter, I was therefore rather curious to see what we would be able to offer each other. For me, it was like breaking new ground. As it turned out, she managed to break through the mother's powerful 'protective sheath' much faster than my son and thus she became more accessible to me. The soft tenderness of the little creature in my arms appealed to my protective instincts. I felt that with this frail infant I needed to be very attentive to every gesture. For at this age, any verbalized form of expression would not be accessible to her, which made all the unspoken forms of communication all the more important.

Soon it seemed to me that the things I discovered with my little daughter were in fact also 're-discoveries', as she enabled me to retrieve a softer, more loving and understanding attitude which turned out to be beneficial as a counterpart to a tough, critical masculine side. To the extent to which I am able to develop my protective qualities with the little girl, I am also able to be more tender with myself.

The challenges I have to meet with my five-year-old son are of a very different nature. He was very close to me from the onset and almost felt like a smaller edition of myself. Despite this, it took me longer to meet him or to come close to him at the soul level. Now it seems to me that he had to use his mother to defend against my rather huge transference. The great physical resemblance was like an invitation to identify with him, to jump on his bandwagon as it were, in order to share at least in imagination his unlimited potential for growth on the one hand and, on the other, to expect that he would reincarnate some personal traits and carry on the family tradition. Now he manages to defend himself against such huge demands in different ways. Playfully, but so that all notice, he'll pummel me forcefully with his little fists and ask "Who is stronger?" Or he'll get on a chair and then on the table and want to know "Who is bigger?" This little game forced me to sit down and think. It made me question my own attitude and generated respect for my son's way of being.

Just as I rediscover the feminine part of my soul, my *anima*, through my daughter, my wife learned to live a new potential in herself through our son. It was amazing to see his clearly masculine play interests which were clearly not initiated by us. It meant that my wife had to learn how to play at model car racing and at how to raise loads as high as possible with toy cranes. Considering her clearly feminine motherly nature, these games were rather alien to her. But in the end she found them stimulating and enriching. This confrontation with the masculine, possibly her *animus*, found expression in completely new forms in her work as a potter.

In my daily life as a child therapist, I experience myself as a catalyst to such changes. Parents entrust their children to me for examination and treatment. However, it never takes long before it becomes apparent that—usually without realizing it—the child's mother or parents also need me to confide in. The child is sent ahead as a pioneer as it were to reconnoitre the new territory. I think this is perfectly legitimate, for I know how much of a struggle the parents may go through before they manage to entrust their child to a specialist, no doubt because they sense or know somehow that ultimately they are concerned at least as much as the child. It is probably for the same reason that parents follow their child's therapy with such rapt attention or suspicion, as the case may be.

A mother called me after a few sessions with her son, very worried to find out what I had been doing with him. Apparently he had suddenly turned unusually plucky and impertinent; before, he had always been good and obedient. This wasn't worth paying a lot of money for! Secretly, I was very pleased, of course, that something had started to move. Obviously the therapy hours had afforded the boy some relief, possibly because at my place, removed from the influence of the family, he was finally able to be himself. The parents suspected that as a result the ball was again in their own court and it worried them. They almost broke off the boy's therapy. In the course of a very patient talk which I had with the parents, they managed to intimate that in their own way both of them were in considerable trouble. Subsequent talks with the mother took her back to her own unhappy childhood. It turned out that *she* was the child looking for help. Much later she sent to me a little essay entitled 'Our son's therapy: Shame or opportunity?' Even the parents' relationship received new impulses as a result of the experience.

This simple example is only one of many. All of them demonstrate the children's important role as eye-openers for their parents. The communicating tubes which we know from physics provide a very appropriate image for this process. The changes take place in all parts of the system. As a result, a new equilibrium is established in the system as a whole, provided that the system is not stopped-up. The children's psychological disturbances, their *symptoms*, are therefore significant for the parents and the family as a whole. They have the purpose of triggering off changes and point to the new directions to be taken. Far from all the parents are able to avail themselves of this opportunity. Anxiously they dig in behind their defensive bastion, thus preventing their child's 'message' from reaching them. In fact, they seem to be intent on making every effort to see to it that nothing changes about the arrangement that has been working for so many years.

Looking back, it turned out to be the most difficult children who were able to get the message across to their parents and bring about changes. The first-born often pave the way for their siblings who are then able to thrive and sail onto the wind of the eldest as it were. Parents with 'modern' ideas are inclined to be too devoted and attentive to their children while neglecting their own needs. Children of such parents will find it difficult to develop their own personality. Both parents and children will have trouble discovering their own individuality. In this respect too, it seems to me more important to be 'adequate' as a parent rather than 'ideal'.

Puberty is overwhelming not merely for the young person in question, but also for the parents. Everything seems to be out of tune, even in a family where life had been previously harmonious. This was, no doubt, at the origin of the initiation rites practiced by primitive populations. These rites are public celebrations during which not only is the adolescent promoted to manhood after undergoing dramatic trials, but the parents are also made to suffer great pains while the village community experiences the rite as a renewal and reminder of the original tribal culture.

Parents of adolescent daughters and sons have usually reached mid-life, a time of incipient decline in the normal course of affairs, insofar as they are prepared to accept this perspective. It is an occasion for some critical retrospection; and, at this very critical stage, the child goes through puberty, unsparingly questioning himself, God and the world and most of all his parents. More than at any other time, the children now go their own way, following their own nose. 'I never took the liberty of doing a thing like that at your age', parents are heard to say, while looking at this newly found freedom partly outraged and partly with surreptitious envy.

These children awakening to adulthood seem to be intent on shaking off their parents. More than anything, they probably try to rid themselves of the parents' heavy expectations and needs for self-fulfillment. If they are successful, the parents have to take back all of the projections and then confront their contents. The more concretely children find and go their own way, the more painfully the parents become aware that they must also go theirs, which may come as a relief in some way. Indeed they may have neglected it or never dared to start out like their own children.

Faced with what they consider to be their 'ungrateful' children, many parents begin to wonder about the meaning of their own lives, no doubt especially if they did or sacrificed 'everything' for their child, placing all their hopes in their children instead of themselves. In cases where a daughter, for example, launches into a somewhat multifaceted love life, despite her parents moral principles, or a son intended for a university career is satisfied with some modest apprenticeship or manual trade, despite the high-level education he has received, few parents are capable of accepting such a turn-about as to accept their children's need to go their own way and to find their own identity. Few are the parents who are able to discern aspects of their own unlived life in the direction taken by their children and to draw the conclusions for the way they want to live the second part of their life in order to round out their own personality. Special efforts are required of parents whose children have not been going astray in their lives, but are overtaken by an accident or a deadly disease. I always recall the general powerlessness and speechlessness of parents and medical and nursing staff when it became impossible to arrest a malignancy to save a child. I also used to feel taxed to the utmost whenever all the available medical therapy, intended for active change, failed me miserably. Along with the parents, I became a silent and deeply moved witness to the amazing inner knowledge these children possessed, indeed, the wisdom which managed to guide up to some extent or even to change some of us. These children were my most important teachers: I learned to listen actively instead of handling, manipulating the situation, to change myself rather than wanting to produce change. Only such an attitude makes it possible to allow things to take the course they have to: to put into effect the inner life plan, coming closer to what Jungian psychology calls the 'Self'.

Sick children, difficult children, and ultimately my own children have brought about fundamental changes in myself. I am grateful to them because they have helped me to come closer to my true nature.

However, the more we insist on changing children, the greater the chances that our expectations will be doomed. It is much more important for us to respect the laws of nature which we cannot control. Man may have become tremendously powerful as a result of his technological knowledge and skills. Before long everything may seem to be within his reach. It is no trouble for him to destroy life. But he cannot create it. His efforts to protect and allow life hinge on constant readiness to change.

Inasmuch as we are human and therefore imperfect, we shall never be able to do perfect justice to this challenge. At the same time it would be very hard on children to have 'perfect' parents who have mastered everything. For the children, such parents would be unattainable and insuperable, and a cause for miserable failure in life. As a result, some of the burden always needs to be passed on for our children to carry.

The Body as Mirror:
Psychosomatics in Childhood
and Adolescence

I do not regard psychosomatic illnesses as a new, additional category of diseases of children and adolescents, as, so to speak, a new
subspecialty, which might even require a new kind of specialist. I
wonder if the term 'psychosomatic' does justice to the reality.
Isn't any disease psychosomatic? Are there illnesses in which the
psyche does not take part? Or the reverse, are there those which
the body does not 'feel'? In this regard, the term 'psychosomatic'
stands in the way of an integral, holistic conception of man and
his illnesses.

Psychic or somatic? This becomes a moot question when one
realizes that the course of every illness, however physical, is always psychologically conditioned to a substantial degree. When
the will to live is lacking, a relatively harmless disease can become
life-threatening.

The field of so-called psychosomatic illnesses is large and difficult to delimit: what about cancer, where we discuss more and
more psychic contributing factors? Or what about schizophrenia,
where physical factors seem possible, metabolic as well as ana-
tomical? The field includes not only physical conditions with a
psychological basis, but also mental suffering which has its source
in a bodily process; such reactions might be called 'somato-
psychic'. But this distinction again proves to be a hindrance to an
expanded concept of physical and psychological unity. The need
for systemic classification is in keeping with the exact, scientific
training which characterizes us as doctors. But more frequently it
turns out that this training does not correspond to reality, particularly in the interrelationship of psyche and soma.

When we speak of illnesses, we must also speak of healths,
which would emphasize the distinct character of the health of the
individual. Each of us is on the way to his own health, which

cannot be a statistically recorded norm, and which must not be described as the absence of disease, but rather as a continual interrelationship between health and illness. The two stand together in a fluid balance. Is health possible without illness? Does illness not lead one closer to health, that is, to the experience of wholeness? Many convalescents experience an inner maturation following severe illness. And parents are included in this experience through their sick children.

Sickness and health as concepts do not deserve the absoluteness with which they are too often endowed. What is sick? What is healthy? It is often very 'healthy' to respond to a particular situation by becoming ill. Who sets the boundaries? What is still healthy? What is already sick? I regard illness as an entirely natural counterpart of health. Sickness and health are in dialogue with one another. Many an illness really makes one healthier (μη δαρεισ ανΘρωποσ ου παιδευεται—who never was shattered will never be taught). Far be it from me to overvalue or to glorify illness. Certainly, illnesses must be taken seriously, as signals of a mistaken or one-sided attitude on the part of the patient.

The Family

The special situation of children and adolescents is characterized by the fact that the parents are more or less closely involved. On the one hand, the illness of a child often expresses something 'unsayable', which is really for the parents to say. On the other hand, such illnesses are valuable messages for the parents, to the extent that they are willing to 'hear' them. The recovery of a child from an illness very often marks a milestone in the parents' separation from the child, as well as in their own development. Must children bear the illnesses for their parents? This seems to occur particularly in families where the parents remain in a deep psychic attachment to, or entanglement with, their children. Viewed against this backdrop, the guilt feelings of parents with sick children may be more understandable.

The question of guilt is a burning one to parents of sick children. This is true even when the doctor takes pains to account for the illness as being 'purely physical'. I think it is important to acknowledge these deeply-rooted feelings as an essential, vital step in the development of the parents together with their sick children. We should not attempt to explain them away with factual statements.

The Illness as Shadow

Dealing with psychosomatic illnesses is a way of striving for wholeness. This category of diseases at the boundary between body and soul reminds us of a split in our patients and our families. But in the illness itself lies the energy to bridge the gap and to unify two aspects of the total personality that have become opposites.

Seen psychologically, being sick is an especially visible and tangible confrontation with the 'shadow', that is, with the qualities in us which have been hidden, neglected, and condemned to a degrading shadow life. Often one realizes that these qualities led to an illness just because they were unrecognized. Viewed in this way, illnesses can be compared to dreams, which also have the function of reminding us of hidden, forgotten aspects of ourselves. Like dreams, they provide an opportunity to raise these 'sunken treasures'. The convalescent can then fruitfully incorporate these rediscovered qualities. Thus one can consider recuperation as an integration of the shadow.

Our treatment of disease is similar to our dealings with the shadow. We see both as an unwelcome disruption, to be eliminated as soon as possible. Our entire system of medicine, clinics, medications and health insurance is shaped by this attitude. We have a Sickness Disposal System which ignores the energies hidden within illness instead of making use of them. By declaring organs sick and entrusting them to the specialists, we and the specialists risk amputating the organ, so to speak. When we cut ourselves off from the sick portion of ourselves, we sever our connection to that very portion of ourselves which has something essential to 'say'.

In working with children, we see the impressive potential for physical health which is natural to them. There are impressive potentials for health in mental, psychosomatic illnesses as well as in physical diseases of children. The wise doctor knows that he does not heal the child; rather, he only creates the best possible conditions for the child to attain his or her own healing. This is in complete accord with the age-old expression, *medicus curat, natura sanat*, 'the doctor cures, Nature heals'.

When we experience the development a child undergoes in the process of becoming ill, being ill, and recovering, our respect for this illness grows, and we would wish for the child that all his illnesses would not be in vain. Is it this power of recovery which gives parents legitimate reason to let their children become sick (instead of, and for, the parents themselves)? In this light, children appear as pioneers who can lead the parents on a path to health, that is, to human wholeness.

When we meet the ill person in this spirit, we learn to respect his illness as a self-expression, a self-portrait, comparable to a drawing. Through such phrases as 'she took ill', 'he broke his leg', or in German, 'er erkältete sich' ('he caught cold'), our speech reveals that such conditions do not come to us from the outside, from out of nowhere, but rather that our psyche participates in them.

The Environment

We could view psychosomatic illness today in the larger context of man's troubled environment: the ecological structure of the environment reacts sensitively to our one-sided intrusions into its balance. "Nature has shown us that she is still there," concluded a local politician recently as he looked at the damage in his region resulting from a catastrophic thunderstorm. There was a faint note that he was thinking also of an underlying provocation at man's hand, as if to say: 'Nature does not permit rape; when we abuse her too much she rises up in revolt'.

Although Nature can be seen as a model for teaching us about the disturbed human organism, the reverse is also true. Man can give the environment the benefit of his knowledge of his own body. The experience of wholeness which the ill person has in his encounter with illness, and which we can have in our encounter with him, holds valuable impulses for our interactions with the world and the environment. Sick children not only point out the disunity in their organisms and in their families; they also supply the attentive physician with some components for healing that disunity.

I do not wish to condemn the modern world as hostile to children nor to glorify previous centuries; in earlier epochs, in many places and often enough, the plight of children was far worse than today. The fact that the rights of children, indeed even their very existence, are perceived and acknowledged can be described as a great achievement of this century. Although it is impossible for us to change the past, it seems all the more important to me to point out conditions in the environment of children today which foster illness. To briefly summarize my diagnosis, we are looking now for niches: niches in which children can play freely in harmony with their inner images; in which they can discover and try out their gifts and potentials; in which adolescents can live out the primeval pattern of crisis and transformation, that is, where their archetypal anticipations can be fulfilled.

Symptom and Synchronicity

It is often too simplistic to see a physiological process as caused by a psychological condition. Rather there is a complex interaction, or even a more or less meaningful coincidence, in the sense of a synchronicity.

What is synchronicity? What is a symptom? The more I try to understand both, the more I see how closely connected they are. 'Symptoma' is Greek and means that something falls together with something else. Applied to psychosomatic events the meaningful coincidence occurs between an inner subject and an outer object (psyche and physis, mind and body, child and environment). And there is a third factor: the symptom, that seems to be equally correlated to the inner and the outer, but not in a causal and explainable way.

When we respect the archetypal or transpersonal aspect of psychosomatic events, we are better prepared to deal with them. We do not try to treat the symptom away, but rather we acknowledge it as a leading sign, a guide in the further life journey of the afflicted person. The synchronistic quality of the symptom may explain the puzzling fact that the more logically we try to analyze the psychosomatic symptoms and the more rationally we treat them, the more we fail in our healing effort. The more we know, the more we know nothing.

It matters not so much *what* we do in therapy, but *how* we do it. We must make room for that third transpersonal element in our work. A symptom is like an oracle: we must consult it in order to make a diagnosis. And then we must provide space so that the Self can manifest. This is the creative or, I dare to say, the religious aspect of our work.

Death and Transformation

Introduction

Involvement with the dying demands a confrontation with one's own views on the subject of death, which must be based on personal experience. It is not the intention of this work to present a general examination of this wide topic, but instead to place its emphasis on the point where personal experience and the wealth of knowledge offered by C.G. Jung's analytical psychology may contribute to the many diverse areas of work with the dying. Yet it not dying which is in the foreground of these reflections, but death. For so long as Death is lurking in the background, he casts a shadow even more menacing and paralyzing over the whole field.

". . . death is a faithful companion to the human being, following him as his shadow; one has yet to understand how much the will to live equates to the will to die," wrote Jung (1972a, 56) in a short letter of condolence to a friend. In our world, stripping off this shadow and banishing death from our daily thought seems to be a tireless pursuit. And yet from the point of view of Jungian thought, we cannot separate death from its larger context, from a unity: death is not only part of the whole, but it could provide the culmination, even the perfecting, of a fulfilled life.

The lives of nature and of man are interwoven with passing over and dying. Daily patterns and yearly cycles provide us with familiar pictures of this: we speak of the evening, the autumn of life. Day in, day out, we are reminded of dying—the separation from a loved one, the farewell to a stage of life. Every decision is a rehearsal for death.

Medical duty to a human being always contains within itself, however hushed and far in the background, a confrontation with death. "The medic of antiquity, who was almost always a man of science and a philosopher at the same time, meditated with a skull on his desk. He did not perceive death from the point of view of life. He perceived life through the orbital cavities of the skull" (Hillman 1966, 46). Especially in the second half, the afternoon, of life, death becomes an integral task, even the goal, of the process of rounding-out and becoming whole, which Jung called "individuation". This is why there cannot be an independent discipline of, or specialist in, therapy for the dying. Moreover, the attention of the person who accompanies the dying cannot be directed solely to the last phase of life, when for the most part everything has gone by. Instead, in these last moments one may experience a constellation of the whole of life. To a great extent, the quality and fulfillment of a life is determined by the quality of death—the ability to die. Life and death are contained within one another.

Soul and Death

> The atmosphere of death is the most frightening of all
> feelings. An elemental force appears. You're just thrown off
> track . . . I loathe death.

These are the thoughts of an adolescent analysand, whose terrible uncertainty about the purpose of life led him to contemplate suicide. He described to me in vivid detail how this cruel and yet sublime occurrence shook him down to his very roots. He had been confirmed, a weak procedure which supplants earlier initiation rites. In its modernity and level-headedness, confirmation was unable to provide him with the powerful symbolism of death and transformation which we find in the puberty rites of some native tribes (Eliade 1958), or of death and resurrection as found in the Christian tradition (Holy Week). Is it a coincidence that this boy kept a dejectedly low profile, particularly during this celebration, such that the worried minister approached me about him? When the celebration, according to this minister, had been deliberately kept sober and low-key? In therapy, this boy was able to come through his 'death', and a transformation was made possible by the sustaining symbolism of the images drawn from his unconscious, his dreams, drawings and sandplays (Kiepenheuer 1984).

Questions about the meaning of life, about death and about an afterlife are as ancient as the history of man. Mythologies and religions give evidence of man's struggle for answers. Again and again, the point of departure for this search lies in the experience of a profound abyss. The terror of death as a motivating point of origin is visibly expressed by the present funeral rites of many primitive tribes (in Malaysia, Laos, and Sumatra). We hear of these tribes that they let the dead lie where they have died. They flee, without ever returning to that place if they can avoid it (Herzog 1960, 21). Only actual burial rites are a sign of a differentiated ritual confrontation with the numinosity of death. Modern civilization, on the other hand, provides us with technical means to help us to veil death and avoid confrontation with it. Rites which have been with us since ancient times, "expressions of archetypal expectations" (Jung, 1972b, 440), are threatened with atrophy. Symbols which were capable of accompanying the human being through the important stages of life are fading (cf. Fierz 1982, 120) .

An 'afterlife' or 'beyond' remains hidden to us in living human perception. No one can prove that anything other than nothingness awaits us after death. No human being has ever returned after having crossed death's threshold. When asked about his faith in a 'beyond', Jung described himself as "as unassuming as an earthworm" (Jung 1972 p. 306). Jung did not believe; he adhered to whatever he was able to comprehend with his human senses. Any further speculation he treated with utmost caution. Asked about his opinion as to life continuing after death, he replied in this same letter:

> Actually this question exceeds the capacity of the human mind, which cannot assert anything beyond itself. Furthermore, all scientific statements are merely probable. So we can only ask: is there a probability of life after death? The point is that, like all our concepts, time and space are not axiomatic but are statistical truths. This is proved by the fact that the psyche does not fit entirely into these categories. It is capable of telepathic and precognitive perception. To that extent it exists in a continuum outside time and space.

Even in his dissertation Jung had turned towards those strange phenomena later to be summed up under the heading of parapsychology. He thought of these phenomena mainly as an expression of the objective psyche, lifting them into "relative spacelessness and timelessness" (Jung 1976, 453).

There are plenty of indications that at least part of the human soul is not subject to the laws of space and time, to our three-dimensional world, to the limitations of time and to our rational understanding. Whoever dreams is astonished by the freedom with which our dreams pass beyond the laws of rational comprehension; at the twist of a finger a scene changes, the dead come alive, the future becomes foreseeable. And it is amazing "how little fuss the unconscious soul makes about death" (1976, 976).

Throughout history man has known many accounts which, often independent of each other, attribute such transcendental qualities to the soul. Three of these, representative of many others, will be cited here, from very different sources:

1. A personal account: C. G. Jung's Vision;
2. A survey: 'encounters' with the dead;
3. A mythological tradition: the Tibetan Book of the Dead.

Jung's Vision
Jung's own attitude to death underwent a major transformation due to a dangerous illness when he was 69, and due to the pictures which came to him during that crisis.

> At the beginning of 1944 I broke my foot, and this misadventure was followed by a heart attack. In a state of unconsciousness I experienced deliriums and visions which must have begun when I hung on the edge of death and was being given oxygen and camphor injections. The images were so tremendous that I myself concluded that I was close to death. My nurse afterwards told me, "It was as if you were surrounded by a bright glow." That was a phenomenon she had sometimes observed in the dying, she added. I had reached the outermost limit, and do not know whether I was in a dream or an ecstasy. At any rate, extremely strange things began to happen to me.
>
> It seemed to me that I was high up in space. Far below I saw the globe of the Earth, bathed in a gloriously blue light . . .
>
> I had the feeling that everything was being sloughed away, everything I aimed at or wished for or thought, the whole phantasmagoria of earthly existence fell away or was stripped from me—an extremely painful process. Nevertheless something remained; it was as if I now carried along with me everything I had ever experienced or done, everything that had happened around me. I might also, say, it was with me, and I was it. I consisted of all that, so to speak. I consisted of my own history, and I felt with great certainty: this is what I am. 'I am this bundle of what has been, and what has been accomplished.'
>
> This experience gave me a feeling of extreme poverty, but at the same time of great fullness. There was no longer anything I wanted or desired. I existed in an objective form; I was what I had been and lived. At first the sense of annihilation predominated, of having been stripped or pillaged; but suddenly that became of no consequence. Everything seemed to be past; what remained was a *fait accompli,* without any reference back to what had been. There was no longer any regret that something had dropped away or been taken away. On the contrary: I had

everything that I was, and that was everything. (Jaffé 1962, 289–291)

What follows is the description of his re-entry into life on Earth. In that situation, this was a deep disappointment to him: "Now I have to fit into the simple, subordinate 'system of boxes' again!" In the following days, wrestling with his illness, he beheld great visions. They reached their peak in the 'Hierosgamos', the sacred marriage of Zeus and Hera, as told by Homer in the *Iliad*::

> ... the 'sweet smell' of the Holy Ghost. This was it. There was a *pneuma* of inexpressible sanctity in the room, whose manifestation was the *mysterium conjunctionis* ...
>
> The objectivity which I experienced in this dream and in the visions is part of a completed individuation. It signifies detachment from valuations and from what we call emotional ties. In general, emotional ties are very important to human beings. But they still contain projections, and it is essential to withdraw these projections in order to attain to oneself and to objectivity. Emotional relationships are relationships of desire, tainted by coercion and constraint; something is expected from the other person, and that makes him and ourself unfree. Objective cognition lies hidden behind the attraction of the emotional relationship; it seems to be the central secret. Only through objective cognition is the real *conjunctio* possible. (Jaffé 1962, 295-97)

A fruitful period of work began for Jung after this illness, as well as an unconditional "Ja-sagen zum Sein", saying 'Yes!' to being, as he called it. In a letter he expressed his newly-won attitude in this way:

> ... the *aspectus mortis* is a mighty lonely thing, when you are stripped of everything in the presence of God. One's wholeness is tested mercilessly. (Jung 1972b 450)

In more recent times, accounts of the experiences of people who have almost died have been published, which correspond impressively to Jung's account (Moody 1975; Hampe 1975; Wiesenhütter 1978). Common to most of these experiences is that the person leaving the physical bounds retains the power of perception and observes his own lifeless body. There is frequent mention of a light which seems to receive the dying person; it is felt to be offering shelter and warmth. The dying experience something like a high-speed review of their lives, posing the critical question of whether their task in life has been fulfilled. Moving back into the re-animated body is described by the survivors as laborious or even tormenting.

Encounters with the Dead

In her book *Apparitions and Precognition,* Aniela Jaffé gives a psychological interpretation and commentary on the extensive material about border experiences. It stems from 1,200 written replies to a survey conducted by the periodical *Schweizerische Beobachter,* dating back to 1954 and 1955. The replies came from all segments of the population. Jaffé points to the treasure of collective knowledge which found expression here, and to the strength of the value of these border experiences for the persons involved. The letters are about dreams, visions, and apparitions in which the dying seem to be attracting the notice of the living, often at a time when physical death had not yet set in and was not yet foreseeable. Most of these meetings of the soul seem to have had a calming and comforting effect. In this way, death is portrayed in many of the accounts as the homecoming of a person to 'his people,' to 'the fathers.' The apparitions of the spirits of the familiar dead are often described as being surrounded by a radiating, touching, gladdening glow. Here is an example of such a letter:

> One night I saw my dear father drifting past me, surrounded by a shining light. Thought I was dreaming at first, but then sat up in bed. So I was completely awake. We looked into each other's eyes; father was beautiful, more than I had ever seen him before; I'd almost say, he looked transfigured. Then the thought occurred to me—something had surely happened to my father. The next day I received a telegram: father had died of a heart attack. Aged 85.—Had always been a bit worried about my father's spiritual life, but because I saw him so beautiful, I figured he must have been prepared inwardly. That gave me great satisfaction . . . (Jaffé 1978, 69)

This quotation encourages me to entrust the reader with a very personal experience, my father's death, which affected me very deeply, but which opened up new paths at the same time.

> During a study visit in London, an indescribable restlessness suddenly took hold of me. It was my birthday, and I had been invited to coffee and cake at Susan Bach's home (vide bibliography). She was helping me at that time to an understanding of spontaneous drawings by terminally ill children. I hurried back to my flat, where I almost immediately received a telephone call, telling me of my father's death from a heart attack suffered during a visit to the sun observatory high in the mountains of

Mexico. He had been an astronomer of the sun, and had always spoken of 'his sun' with visible passion. I later discovered a small book with many woodcuts in it, next to his bed at home. It was called *Die Sonne* (Masereel 1947). On page in particular was marked with a piece of paper. This picture seemed to me to indicate my father's presentiment of his death. It was only afterwards that I learned something about an old Mexican myth in which there is the concept of the dying uniting with the sun. But apart from this collective aspect, I felt the death of my father to be a personal message to me, since he had 'chosen' my birthday for his 'homecoming to the sun.' Many times since we have come face to face in dreams, where he has developed a kind, paternal tenderness which would have been impossible to realize during his lifetime.

Figure 21 *The Sun (woodcut)*

These accounts show, in a varied and verifiable way, the quality of soul which Jung describes, the "relative spacelessness and timelessness". The encounters with the apparitions do not in any way explain the mystery of death, as Jaffé rightly states, but they can reduce the fear of it.

In his essay 'Synchronicity: An Acausal Connecting Principle' (in *Collected Works,* Volume VIII), Jung devotes himself extensively to the nature of these apparitions, in terms of their meaning to the person to whom they occur. And, in a letter to Professor H. Bender, he wrote:

> The psychologist, who is concerned with the processes in the unconscious, knows that these remarkable 'chances' happen chiefly when archetypal conditions are present, and it looks as if the inner psychic disposition were reflected either in another person or in an animal or circumstances generally, thanks to a simultaneous and causally independent parallel disposition. Hence the accompanying phenomena in cases of death: the clock stops, a picture falls off the wall, glass cracks, etc. (Jung 1972b, 415)

Jung's term 'synchronicity' refers to the concurrence of two or more events which, to the person concerned, have a profound coherent meaning, while they could not be explained by ordinary cause and effect. One would commonly say, 'Oh, what a coincidence!' Other mysterious occurrences, such as telepathy, visions, ghosts, and other extraordinary precognitions also belong to the field of coincidence. While an objective, physical investigation of these events contributes little toward clarification, we can look at them from the perspective of the subject, as a projection of deep archetypal contents. In these, the Self frees mysterious inner powers which transcend the principle of simple causality in the outer world, and which break through the limitations of space and time. The concept of synchronicity views inner and outer happenings as meaningfully, albeit not causally, related. For the person concerned, such synchronistic phenomena are in the nature of a numinous event, even a revelation. If they are 'understood,' they can be decisive for the further unfolding of his life.

The Tibetan Book of the Dead
Representative of the numerous testimonies in human history of an existence outside of space and time, let us here consider the *Tibetan Book of the Dead.* (Evans-Wentz 1971)

This volume is a written record from a pupil of a Tibetan

teacher, and is for us an invaluable source of collective, archetypal contents. Jung wrote a foreword and psychological commentary for the German translation. The book contains the instructions read aloud to the dying and the dead on their journey through the four steps of the Bardo state, or 'crossing,' and finally, instructions in preparation for the other world. The deceased is urged to be fully attentive at every stage of the journey. In the first phase he finds out:

> Oh, (so-and-so) of noble birth, listen. You will now experience the Radiation of the Clear Light of Pure Reality. Recognize it . . . Your own Spirit in now the Void, but not to be thought of as the Void of Nothingness, but as a pure Spirit, unrestrained, radiant, blissful is the true consciousness, the all-bountiful Buddha . . . (Evans-Wentz, 170)

At the next stage,where the consciousness steps out of the body, the dead person is made aware of the freedom attained, while the lama reads. From here on, the book is concerned with an increasing detachment from what has been left behind, and with encounters with "peaceful and furious godheads".

The last stage of Bardo leads through the nightworld of death, where the deceased is capable of unrestricted movement, without any special limitations, in any desired bodily shape. In this phase of the 'between,' the deceased is prepared for a terrible "judgement:"

> . . . then a fury of the Death god throws a rope around your neck and pulls you away; she cuts off your head, takes out your heart, tears out your innards, licks out your brains, drinks your blood, eats your flesh and gnaws at your bones . . . even when your body is cut into pieces, it recovers . . . (Evans-Wentz, 245)

The deceased is now exhorted to hold out until he reaches complete deliverance and illumination. The task of the dead person is to fight his karmic inclination toward a new earthly birth: a reincarnation of this kind would be the way of the weak, who are unable to cast off affection and dislike (compare this with Jung's comment on his vision above). Instead, as the deceased is instructed face to face, the last noble goal "would be to enter into" a birth beyond the natural, into a paradisiacal, realm.

In the introduction to the *Tibetan Book of the Dead* we read: ". . . the message of this book is that the art of dying is as vital as the art of living; it complements and crowns it; furthermore, the future existence perhaps depends entirely on a death well mastered . . ." The dying person is taken by the hand, so to speak, with pedagogical patience and skill. Above all, it is not a matter of a farewell to this world, but an introduction, an initiation, into a new, elevated understanding of things. As with every true initiation, the phase of torment and purification is unavoidable; here it is in the nature of Purgatory. An essential feature of this initiation is described by Jung in his forward:

> . . . no process of becoming whole (individuation) is spared this dangerous passage through [the torture], since what is feared also belongs to the whole of the self, the world over and under the dominants of the soul from which the ego has once liberated itself to some extent toward a more or less illusionary freedom . . . (Jung, *Collected Works*, Volume XI)

and, in another place:

> . . . the whole book is drawn from the archetypal contents of the unconscious . . . [Behind these lies the] reality of psychic entities . . . the dead man has to realize . . . that the soul and the giver of all entities are one and the same thing: . . . the world of gods and spirits is 'nothing but' the collective unconscious within me . . . (Jung, *Collected Works* Volume XI)

It is not a question of rationally reducing the godly to a purely psychological phenomenon. On the contrary, the aim of these teachings is to ". . . restore the deity of the soul lost in birth" (Jung, ibid.).

The wisdom presented here, which comes from the collective unconscious of an individual and a people, can prove helpful as an orientation for those looking for a picture of an 'afterlife'. This is all that can be expected of such testimonies. An acceptance of death as an integral part of the journey towards individuation is something which must be acquired by each individual.

Working with the Dying

An essential experience for me in my understanding of death and the dying was my medical work in a ward for children with leukemia or tumors. Many of these children (by no means all) died within months or years of the outbreak of the illness (Hitzig and Kiepenheuer 1976; Kiepenheuer 1978; 1980).

Initially, I suffered from my helplessness in dealing with these children when I believed I ought to do something; and from my speechlessness when I thought it necessary to say something. It was only later that I learned from the children themselves that what mattered was quite different: that is, to be there, to listen and follow them emotionally. This seemed to be a hard thing to do, particularly when there was nothing to be done or said. On these occasions I considered it important to admit to my own helplessness and speechlessness, to accept it, and to bear it.

The two accounts of encounters with terminally ill children which follow are a frank avowal of how I myself was affected. Both children suffered from the same illness: acute lymphatic leukemia. And yet their personalities and their ways of coping with the threatening situation were fundamentally different. These children represented important developments in my own life, in my attitude to death and dying and, therefore, to living. It turned out, as I listened attentively and followed closely their experiences, that the two children became the masters and I, their pupil.

'Elisabeth'

When eight-year-old Elisabeth had to be hospitalized under suspicion of leukemia, I was the head of her ward. The diagnosis was soon confirmed. During three weeks of intensive treatment she occupied a single room, in order to protect her from infections. In a disturbing way this room was sacred to me. Each time I entered I had to give myself a little push to cross the threshold. For me, Elisabeth was marked, destined for a very particular journey a long way ahead of me, accompanied by a sense of distant loneliness, separated even from her family. Although her parents visited her often and brought plenty of presents with them, they seemed to be disconcerted and ill at ease. They spoke only of everyday matters with Elisabeth. Inwardly, they were at a great distance from her. And Elisabeth seemed to wrap herself in a sort of protective mantle which only allowed for superficial contact, as if she did not want her soul to be touched. This presented an added difficulty in visiting her room. There were things on the tip of my tongue which she would not allow me to speak of in conversation. Yet at the same time, to talk of other matters with her seemed too banal, even unworthy of so tragic a fate.

Elisabeth got over her first onset very well. She was in a good strong state when she was discharged. She went to school; friends visited her at home. Externally, it was as though nothing had happened. She came to the outpatient department at regular intervals for treatment and check-ups. This was something that she loathed doing, and she could voice her discontent at great volume. It was these consultations, after all, which tore her out of her day-to-day life, in which she fancied herself completely healthy and normal. Everyone in her environment—parents, older brother and younger sister—did his or her best to stress a healthy, ordinary way of life. A well-meaning medical colleague also devoted herself to the positive in this sense, and undertook things with Elisabeth which accentuated active, vital life and belied the painful reality. Elisabeth greatly appreciated being able to go riding (for example) with her doctor. But a fundamental part of the whole truth was strictly omitted in this arrangement. There existed something of a conspiracy of silence in Elisabeth's world.

Both parents felt a great need to talk about their personal afflictions. We invited them to parents' meetings, where they had an opportunity to share their personal problems with us and with other parents in similar situations. Their marriage had been at the breaking point for many years, and it was only the grave illness of their child which brought them together for the time being, in a kind of emergency partnership. Where Elisabeth was concerned, both tried their utmost to disguise the marital rift and to ignore the menacing illness.

With our encouragement Elisabeth produced many drawings during that time. For many weeks she kept to the same theme: a girl standing under a big umbrella on the edge of the pavement. Huge raindrops fall on the umbrella and collect on the ground into two puddles. A cross-walk is indicated on the street. The girl's head and the upper half of her body are sheltered and hidden under the enormous umbrella. Neither the raindrops nor the glances of others can reach her face.

This picture was a plain expression of her attitude, which I had to accept. She avoided me and would hardly let me get near her. Instead, time and time again she gave me a drawing of this kind, as if to say, 'Leave me alone in my solitude!' Only the crosswalk hinted at an access for me to approach her.

One day her father came to talk to me, when he could hardly bear the persistent silence about the child and her illness any longer. I encouraged him to speak openly with Elisabeth, perhaps during a walk, about his terrible fears and worries, in order to free them both from the awful loneliness of their knowledge. To my great regret this attempt also failed: Elisabeth became indignant as soon as her father began to speak about the illness. She implored him to forget it and to look toward 'normal' things. "What's wrong with you today?" she entreated him, "Why can't you please, please be like you were yesterday and all the days

Figure 22 *The Umbrella (drawing)*

before?" She even shouted the words. Parents, brother, and sister all adhered to this precept from then on, relieved on the one hand, dejected on the other. They carried on with the hollow peace and it seemed to work quite well. But every time Elisabeth had to go to the hospital all hell broke loose. And particularly when she had a relapse she was utterly forlorn. She seemed in no way prepared for it. There reigned an unfathomable stillness about her then. The relapses and complications later returned with increasing frequency and she had to struggle through them in great loneliness.

One day her mother sensed that Elisabeth's life was nearing an end. In a fever, the girl expressed the odd desire, "Give me gravel and sand to eat!" Was it weight she wanted, to hold her securely to the ground? Or had she, in her imagination, already bound herself to the Earth, so soon to claim her? Her mother was completely helpless. She did not know what to do or say. It was beyond her courage to let the girl die at home. Elisabeth was eventually taken to the hospital despite her decided and fervent protests. The sole person able to accompany her in her last hours was her father. Putting his arm around Elisabeth's shoulder, he sensed that he was near to her. Weakly, she repeated her words about gravel and sand, and then firmly clasped her father's hand. He stayed the whole night until she died at dawn. Later he confided in me, telling me that he had only been able to be so close to his dying daughter because he had had the courage to speak so openly with her during that walk. Today, he is very glad that he did.

I had many conversations with the girl's mother during the following months. For her, Elisabeth had not yet died. The painstaking emotional task of reliving and coming to terms with her daughter's death ensued. At that time she spent many hours in the cemetery at her daughter's grave. It took two years before she could let her die inwardly. So long as she disavowed the death she was unable to really live herself and was inaccessible to the demands of her family. Both living children suffered greatly from their mother's affective absence. The father had long since left the house.

This girl's death had raised some painful questions, without providing any answers in relief. What bewildered me perhaps most of all was her immutably affirmative attitude toward life, which seemed to ward off any ominous premonition of dying. I presumed that she felt the inability of her relatives to face the fatal threat and that she respected this loyally.

My wish to share with her the knowledge of her illness in an open conversation remained unfulfilled. There was a tension between the attitude of the girl and my own conviction about sharing death, which I had to endure. It was only after her death that I could use my conviction, to help her mother to catch up, so to speak, with a truth long denied and to open up her own life. If the father had not dared to make the breakthrough for a short moment during the child's lifetime, despite her apparent resistance, she would probably have died in complete loneliness. My accompanying of her dying could, in her lifetime, only be effected through the father.

'Stefan'

My experience with another child, whom I will call Stefan, was quite different. When he was six he acquired acute lymphatic leukemia, which ended his life at the age of nine years and three months.

Stefan was a shy and sensitive child. However, in his regular visits to our outpatient clinic, trust and intimacy gradually developed. It was not so much in words that he expressed them, but in unspoken intimations. His drawings became an important element in our dialogue, and he devoted a great deal of time to them. On Sundays he often got up long before his parents and two brothers to produce new drawings. He brought them to the checkups, at first because I requested it, then later spontaneously. It was very important to him that I should first take notice of the pictures in their entirety, and then I was to describe each one, while he would encourage me to look more closely, correcting or affirming what I said with a nudge, a shake of the head or a nod.

Various favorable circumstances collaborated in my work with the child, his brothers, and his parents. The entire family was rooted in their religious faith. The mother comes from a Spanish Catholic background. The father belongs to the Reformed (Protestant) Church. The parents engaged in lively discussions on religious questions, and included their children in them. With this background, they did not find it difficult to speak with Stefan about his grave illness or to broach the subject of death and an afterlife. They were also able to deal with the questions of their other two sons.

One day, when Stefan had come to the clinic for a check-up, he stood by the windowsill and made the following little drawing using a black ballpoint pen (next page):

In the center of the picture we see a black panther sitting on a rock, ready to jump; on the left is a man armed with a gun. The man's line of sight and the"!" above his head seem to indicate that he may sense the presence of the dangerous animal, but that he is not sufficiently aware of it. What is more, he has no feet, so he cannot even run away! While the panther is surrounded on both sides by the leaves of the bushes, the leaves are missing where the man is standing; perhaps they have already fallen. I refrained from drawing the child's attention to a possible connection between this image and his menacing illness in words. But by the meaningful expression with which he handed me the picture,

Figure 23 *The Panther (drawing)*

I could feel that he was sharing with me and entrusting me with an important part of his inner knowledge.

It is Susan Bach (1966; 1974/5; 1980) that we must thank for learning to value the pictures of our sick children as an important means of expression of their bodily and mental condition. "The child says it in the picture," was the convincing answer to many of our anxious questions. Parents, doctors and nurses were often heard to ask, 'Should I tell the child the whole truth? How should I tell it?' The accurate understanding of the child's drawing often told us only too clearly that the child knew inwardly about the seriousness of the course of events. The question is not whether or how to tell the child, but whether the child will be able to share his inner knowledge with those in his environment. We continue this dialogue with Stefan:

For Mother's Day Stefan took the greatest care in drawing this picture of a fat-bellied Viking ship on rough seas. Ten Vikings are standing on deck, varied in size, color, and armament. All their arms are raised. But only nine shields are there at the disposal of ten men! And we know that Stefan was very particular about his drawings. Six blood-red stripes cover a part of this filled sail. There would be room for about three more stripes on the space which was left white, next to the sixth stripe. Up in the masthead stands an eleventh Viking with a telescope. Seven little strokes over his head probably indicate (in the usual manner of this skillfull draftsman) his sudden attentiveness.

Figure 24 *The Viking Ship (drawing)*

Having duly admired this picture, as always, I ventured to ask Stefan something: "Who is the man up there?" Since I received no reply I asked in another way, "And what does he see through his telescope?" Stefan said, "Another ship." Some weeks later he said of the man in the masthead, "That is you."

One is tempted to relate the strikingly significant numbers here were in Stefan's pictorial 'speech' to biographical dates. If the six blood-red stripes correspond to six years of healthy life and blood, it is possible to estimate how much room there would be left for the ensuing 'white' (leukemic) years. If the ten Vikings have only nine shields, then what happens to the tenth man? Or, translated, 'What happens after nine shielded years, in the tenth, unshielded year?' The further course of Stefan's illness provided an answer in a most unsettling way.

But on the horizon (from an elevated field of vision, so to speak) something new is in sight, something so significant that it is worth seven little strokes to the draftsman. His association of this far-sightedness and fore-sightedness with his doctor is perhaps a sign that he felt himself to be inwardly understood, within our own special dialogue.

After several complications and relapses, the grave course of his illness demanded in-patient treatment in a so-called sterile unit. On a calm morning he drew this picture in the presence of his mother, who was able to look after him in the role of assistant nurse:

Figure 25 *God Looking Down on the Sterile Unit (drawing)*

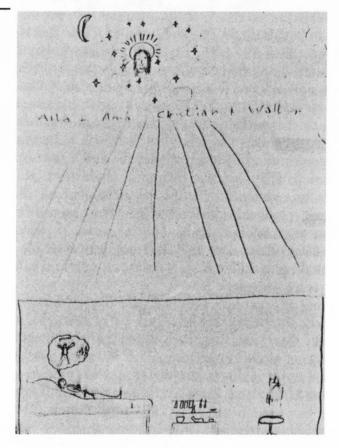

A conversation between Stefan and his mother had preceded the drawing; together they had thought of all the people who were praying for him. He drew with a pencil on a green piece of paper he had chosen himself. Above is God with a halo, surrounded by clouds, stars and the crescent of the waning moon. Below are the names of those most dear to him, and who were praying for him: Mommy, Daddy (in Spanish, his mother tongue) and his brothers. The closed room below is a depiction of his sterile unit. In a bubble above his head is what was probably the content of his prayer, "To be well," and an erect little figure with strong, upraised arms. Next to it is a hand which seems to be pushing away four injections. The mother is sitting at bottom right. She is also praying. Lastly, he drew seven rays between Heaven and the sterile unit.

This is the last picture which Stefan drew. Quite unlike all the earlier pictures, there is nothing here indicating struggle and fighting. A great sense of peace radiates from this picture, which so clearly traces out the child's journey. I understood his prayer, "To be well", in this picture to be meant in the sense of being "delivered, saved, restored" (*salvatus*) The 'man of soul' or the Homunculus, Eidolon (cf. Bach 1974/5, 100), points in the direction of God. The injections pushed to the side might imply, 'Enough injections have been given; they will no longer be needed'. The two worlds, normally so opposed, are bridged by the seven rays in this picture, but they do not quite reach the sterile unit. They remind us of the seven rays above the masthead Viking in the previous drawing. Are these seven rays of significance for the life of the child? Or, alternatively, what are the seven units separating him from Heaven or conducting him to it (as the case may be)?

Let us return to the objective course of his illness. After he had successfully overcome the initial, intense phase of treatment, some disquieting side effects set in. An obscure fever gave increasing cause for concern. None of our measures had any effect on it. Seven days after this drawing, just after his ninth birthday, after three years of illness, Stefan died of a serious lung infection. Both parents were present.

The parents now treasure this drawing like a legacy. Weeks after his death we looked at it again together. In tears, his mother confessed, "Stefan has given us much more than we were ever able to give him." I too was deeply impressed by the inner strength of this dying child. It gave me guidance and support so that I could comfort his family and help other children and their relations. The comfort which can be gained from deep religious conviction is apparent not only in his last drawing, but also in the words he spoke to his parents upon entering the sterile unit: "Jesus has given me so much strength that I will overcome everything that lies ahead."

The family background no doubt plays a formative role in this. Stefan's parents were able to furnish their children with colorful pictures and symbols elucidating their Christian heritage. The fact that these emerge again with all their original force during the last few hours of life indicates that such pictures are prefigured in the deep unconscious and wait only to be rekindled. Only a slight impression of the extent and depth of Stefan's pictorial expression can be given here. Many more drawings came to light after his death, all in all about 300. I spent long evenings going through them together with Stefan's parents. The profundity of their contents convinced us that the life of this child, however short, had come to a well-rounded and fulfilled end.

Other parents with seriously ill or dying children seem also to be aware of a sort of early completion of their children's lives, as when they say, 'This child is different, more mature than the others in an undefinable way.'

Jung said, half to himself, of the impending death of his wife, "She has done enough consciously" (Jaffé 1980, 18). It may have been the comfort of his first-hand experience of this process of becoming whole which moved him to say this.

In the same context, I was struck by a report of a 10-year-old girl who lived for four days after an emergency stomach operation. The child, her consciousness waning, again and again asked her mother (who was nearly always present) to tell the parable of the Good Shepherd or to recite the Twenty-third Psalm, 'The Lord is my Shepherd'.

Later—dying—she summoned her last strength to tell her mother what she was encountering. She saw a meadow full of flowers with many children playing in it, and said at the last, ". . . mother, there he comes now!" And she asked how to touch him: ". . . oh, I know, just like my bridegroom."

In a childishly simple way, the archetypal image of the Hierosgamos had taken shape here. The soul of the child attains wholeness; opposites marry. The child has surely not learned these things. Instead, she was able to activate these contents and draw them up from the deeply embedded consciousness in an hour of profound animation, an *abaissement du niveau mental.*

We come upon this prototype of death as marriage in mythology as well as in the fairy tale. One of the Children's Legends of the brothers Grimm is 'The Heavenly Wedding'. In this tale the poor, starving peasant youth finally betrothes himself to the Virgin Mary and is dead "at the eternal wedding" (Grimm's Fairy Tales).

Perithanatal Care

In creating the expression 'perithanatal care' I am attempting to draw attention to the areas surrounding death, to those involved with the death (Kiepenheuer 1978). Because of the plight of the dying child himself or herself, much else tends to recede into the background and escape our attention. All too often, severely-affected relatives are pushed out of view by the dramatic events. Many parents tend to hide behind silence, out of supposed consideration for the sick child or his or her still-unsuspecting brothers and sisters. Externally they make a display of normality, while inside they are ready to burst into tears. Outsiders admire this apparent composure, calling it 'brave'. But it is really only those who want to avoid confrontation with their own involvement who welcome it.

Accompanying of the Next of Kin

Encounters with dying children have taught us how far ahead the children themselves are of all others, both in their journeys and in their deep knowledge of them. We have also learned that children wish to communicate their knowledge, insofar as they find those near them to be willing and receptive. The collapse of an entire world when a child dies is particularly overwhelming for those 'robbed' parents whose fears had been 'bravely' and successfully concealed. And it is now, when it is they who need extensive guidance and care, that they are further robbed of the familiar proximity of the hospital and of the doctors and nurses who have been close to their child. The medical commitment cannot therefore restrict itself to the patient, or to the time of the acute illness alone. Perithanatal care should encompass the social environment, and include a consideration of the time of its healing, as well.

The is the aim of our parental meetings. For some years now we have been arranging meetings at loose intervals, particularly inviting parents of leukemic children. These evenings give parents an opportunity to speak to the doctors and nurses, not about technical problems, but about those of seemingly minor importance, which are yet central enough to rob many parents of their sleep. A prevailing subject on such evenings is the handling of truths: 'Should I tell my child the truth? And how?' Many parents are guilt-ridden with respect to their sick children. We cannot free them from these feelings, but being able to talk about them brings some relief. Many anxieties about the upbringing of sick children—and healthy ones—are let out into the open. Those attending the meetings particularly value meeting other, similarly afflicted, parents. A feeling of being held and supported within a collective provides a mainstay for many. On rare occasions older brothers or sisters also attend these evenings. Others are sometimes encouraged to come along to the check-ups at the clinic. Many feelings of jealousy or guilt toward the sick member of the family or distrust of the hospital are assuaged in this way.

The parents of deceased children are rarely willing to carry on meeting the parents of those still living. They are afraid of discouraging fragile hopes about the children. We accompany the families whose child has been taken from them by visiting them at home. Our concern in these cases lies in helping them with the task of mourning, allowing a step-by-step withdrawal from the deceased child to occur. We have seen parents who had turned the room of their dead child into a kind of shrine; others had placed the child's urn on the buffet like a sacred relic. It did not occur to them to think about the consequences of such idealizing of the dead child for the surviving children. This glorification went so far in one case that a remaining six-year-old brother did not jump away from a car dashing past. When his mother only just managed to pull him away from the 'accident', the child explained that he wanted to join his brother and go to heaven, as well, since it was so nice there. Fortunately, it was possible in consultations and sand-play therapy to bring parents and child back to Earth and a living purpose: to affirm and cope with the reality of the here and now.

A mother who had lost her first-born son suddenly and unexpectedly informed me of the event by telephone. During a climbing expedition in the middle of summer, he had been caught by sudden snow and both he and his companion had frozen to death. The mother seemed rigid with horror, tormenting herself with guilt. How could I comfort her? The news shook me down to the ground, too. Some years before I had been the boy's therapist over a period of many months. He had always lived on the border of the unreal; he had planned in all seriousness to build an atomically-powered backpack to carry him faster to therapy when his brother was out to poison him ... and so it went. Death in summer snow seemed appropriate to this boy's nature; it was his kind of death. Was that the reason I was so unutterably moved?

Then a person close to me mentioned a novel whose main character dies a gentle death in the snow, very like Hans-Christian Anderson's fairy tale 'The Little Match-Girl'. Unfortunately, I did not have the book on hand. But the same day I received a telephone call from the author's wife. She was entrusting a young, homeless girl to me for consultation. What a remarkable, significant and helpful concurrence! I felt as if my profoundly affected emotions had called up mysterious powers which transcended ordinary probability. And to my mind, such powers were necessary to release the mother from the paralysis of fear. It was only gradually that she became ready to take leave of her son. I accompanied her to the crematorium and was deeply moved by the painful and yet reconciliatory expression which passed over her face when she saw and touched her son for the last time. Later she found records he had left behind, which showed us quite plainly that his death had not been simply a terrible misfortune, but had long been sketched out.

Help for those Helping

He who accompanies the dying must face his own transitoriness—for otherwise his efforts remain ineffectual, academic, and unbelievable. Whenever I witnessed a child dying, the pained helplessness of those around him or her became all too plain to me. They seemed to be too much in need of help themselves to be able to be really near the dying person on his journey. We are here talking about a very essential mission in the life of an individual, a central point in his journey toward becoming whole, his individuation. Jung, in his essay 'Soul and Death', writes: "From mid-life onwards, only he remains alive who is willing to die with life. What happens in the secret hour of life's afternoon is the reversal of the parable, the birth of death . . . Becoming and passing is the same curve . . ." (*Collected Works,* Volume VIII, 447)

1. Training for the Caring

With this helplessness on my mind, I paid particular attention to these helpless, accompanying people, be they nurses, doctors, social workers, teachers or whomever else. My assistance was aimed at making them aware of what dying children know and experience, as the cases above make clear. But it was also intended to encourage them to trust in the knowledge the children possess, and even to allow themselves to be led by it. This seems to be a difficult aim to realize. Some listeners are so apprehensive, so frightened, that they steel their hearts against such an attitude instead of opening up. Few have allowed themselves to become acquainted with their own death and dying, and to incorporate it into their lives. Yet in doing this work, their own existences seem shaken down to the foundations. Frequently they anxiously put off a confrontation with the given, natural reality. In their relation to the dying child they seem to cling to his will to live, and collaborate in trivializing the situation with such remarks as, 'Don't you worry, if you are good and take your tablets you will soon be well again!'

Creative work has proven especially productive in helping us to familiarize ourselves with our own, inborn death. We gave future pediatric nurses a lump of clay or a piece of paper and watercolors, asking them to portray to us what death and dying meant to them. Dealing with the creations which came from their own inner depths repeatedly gave rise to astonishment. It proved to be a good basis for discussion in the small groups which followed. What was particularly surprising was the serene power revealed in these creations, perceived by many with a certain awe. Themes and symbols frequently recurred, but in a variety of arrangements, such as a tree, a flower, a protecting receptacle, a castle or a snail, drawn as a spiral shape culminating in an upward, central point. One of the pictures resulting from the theme 'Death and Dying' depicted a waterfall in the desert. A few flowers line the water before it gradually trickles out and fades away in the dry sand. 'This is how my own life will fade away; nothing remains.' In this way the artist articulated his fear of death. The image invited communal associations and amplifications. Thoughts on the symbolic nature of water led us far from the point of departure. For the artist, the picture of fear turned into a picture of comfort. In the final instance, the comfort rose from his own inner depths. Together, we remembered a poem by Goethe which profoundly corresponded to the inner sentiments this man had gained.

Here is the first verse:

Des Menschen Seele	Man's soul
Gleicht dem Wasser:	Is like water:
Vom Himmel kommt es,	From Heaven it comes,
Zum Himmel steigt es,	To Heaven it rises,
Und wieder nieder	And down again
Zur Erde muss es,	To Earth it must return,
Ewig wechselnd.	Forever alternating.

2. 'The Play of Nature'

Human rational thought has increasingly distanced man from the feeling of being securely bound to nature, and from a sense of belonging to his own, natural origins ('Urnatur'). Man, in his striv-

ing for enlightenment, has raised himself above the eternal patterns and laws. What is the best way for him to reach and regain
them? We find many of these eternal patterns illustrated in nature in unadulterated form. In the dying and germinating of
plants we witness life coming full circle and eternally repeating
itself.

The works of the student nurses, so spontaneously created, already pointed us in this direction. The idea of using nature as a
framework for recovering and representing our own inner nature
sprang from this work. It corresponds to the idea of the play in the
sand, which provides the player—within a smaller compass—
with a protected, but at the same time unrestricting sphere for
play and discovery (vide Kalff 1979).

The International Conference for Jungian Training Candi-
dates, focussing on the subject 'The Conjunction of Opposites'
and lasting one week, provided a forum for such an experiment.
Fourteen of the participants agreed to join in a 'play of nature'
centered around the theme 'Stirb und werde' (die and become)
(Kiepenheuer 1982). First of all we went for a walk, leading us to
unknown surroundings. At a halfway point, a well-lit grove of
birch trees, we sat down in a circle and attuned ourselves to the
subject by way of a few thoughts. Then having gone on to reach
the destination of our walk, a couple of empty, half-demolished
sheep pens at the forest fringe, we collected round a fire. Soon
every one of us, each alone, had found a place within a wide pe-
rimeter of this center in which to find his own interpretation of
'dying and becoming'.

Later, most participants felt the desire to tell the others of the
images, thoughts, feelings, and ideas going through their minds.
The stroll from stop to stop became a moving show of the personal and collective depths of the soul. Here, I will dwell on some
singular, but important and recurring themes in particular:

The Earth, providing shelter and receiving what is dying, but
able also to regenerate and become the seat for new life, was a
motif frequently encountered. For others the nature play became
a meeting with deceased relations whom they experienced as
'kind, oddly comforting'. These relatives, too, paved the way for a
completely new perspective on life. There was also mention of an-
cestral spirits and evil, menacing powers.

Some of the participants called their work an altar on which
something living was sacrificed, but which also—perhaps because of the sacrifice—appeared to be a gateway to another
world. Miraculously, one of the nature players found a folded

piece of paper in front of 'his' dwelling in the mountain solitude. On it was written in a childlike scrawl:"One must not let oneself be confused, but stand by the truth." The man was moved by the contents and the simplicity of these lines. They were of particular relevance to him. But then, it is the mark of 'synchronistic phenomena' that they appear to the person concerned in an original, archetypal setting. For my part, I was impressed with how this man, who had previously struck me as somewhat arrogant and didactic, became pensive and began to radiate a new, genuine simplicity.

The scenes of the nature play had a great impact on our involvement with opposites. The participants did not recoil from dealing with the tension between paired contrasts, like 'Good-Evil', 'Dragon-Shrine', 'Withering-Germinating', 'Life-Death', For some, grappling with these opposites assumed the character of an 'active imagination'. Where opposites interact, energies begin to flow: ". . . here must always be high and low, hot and cold etc., so that the equilibrating process—which is energy—can take place" (Jung, *Collected Works,* Volume VII, 75). Astonishingly, it is precisely this permitting of 'this, and that, too' which can lead toward a way out of the stalemate of 'irreconcilable' opposites, and which can often open up unexpected options or paths. The human journey of individuation aims toward a state of wholeness, toward an acceptance of the inner oppositions and an integration of the forgotten and 'shadow' qualities. However, under the conditions of this life on Earth a total psychic wholeness, or a complete unification of the opposites (*Conjunctio Oppositorum*) can always only be a goal or a direction.

At the end of his 'dying and becoming' fantasies, one of the players in the group expressed this in the following way: ". . . so I felt safe, but perhaps too much so; the division between Life and Death, Good and Evil is still too distinctly plain." He experienced his earthly consciousness, which makes clear distinctions, as a form of safety, but as a limitation at the same time," . . . "the recognition of Good and Evil" will not permit the liberating fusion of opposites. In a letter to a person seeking advice Jung wrote this:

> The phenomenon of life consists of a great many pairs of opposites, there is no energy without opposites. But inasmuch as you share in the opposites you are in conflict at least in a continuous up and down of pain and pleasure. It is certainly desirable to liberate oneself from the operation of opposites but one can

only do it to a certain extent, because no sooner do you get out
of the conflict than you get out of life altogether. So that liberation can be only a very partial one. It can be the construction of
a consciousness just beyond the opposites. Your head may be
liberated, your feet remain entangled. Complete liberation
means death ... (Jung 1972, 247)

One participant allowed the 'togetherness of life and death' to
enter her. "It disturbs me, and to give my irritation a shape, I am
reminded bit by bit of Goethe's 'Seelige Sehnsucht'. Exactly that,
die and live ..." The experience was so overwhelming for the cautious and restrained woman that she was able to recite the poem,
which she had not remembered since her schooldays, with the utmost fervor. The final verse is as follows:

Und solang du das nicht hast,
Dieses: Stirb und Werde!
Bist du nur ein trüber Gast
Auf der dunklen Erde.

(And so long as you haven't this,
This: Die and become!
You are only a dull guest
On the dark Earth.)

For a seeker who did not shrink from the inexpressibility of
death, this nature-play seemed to provide a valuable path. The
frame of nature offered protection and freedom to the individual
to encounter himself and to bring up hidden qualities of the Self,
with the possibility of experiencing them as belonging to the Self.
An atmosphere of the numinous enveloped the participant, in
which deep layers of the unconscious could sound in him. In such
situations, shapes and powers rise to the surface, uniting the individual with the 'Urnatur', his primordial nature, the origin-point
of nature common to all. Jung described this from his own experience in a letter:

Yesterday I had a marvellous dream ... (it) meant a great con-
solation. I am no more a black and endless sea of misery and
suffering but a certain amount thereof contained in a divine
vessel. The situation dubious. Death does not seem imminent,
although an embolism can occur any time again. I confess I am
afraid of a long drawn-out suffering. It seems to me as if I am
ready to die, although it looks to me that some powerful

thoughts are still flickering like lightning on a summer night. Yet they are not mine, they belong to God, as everything else which bears mentioning. (Jung 1972b, 450)

Conclusion

Death is everywhere; he is our 'faithful companion'. He forces us to take a stand. As 'shadow' to life, death is an integral part of the whole. Harmonizing and coming to terms with this part is the goal of the process of becoming whole, of individuation. "The fundamental opposites . . . called body and soul, activity and passivity, spirit and matter, here-and-now and otherworldly . . . are all symbolized in the opposition of life and death" (Hillman 1966, 55). The interaction between these fundamental opposites means confrontation with wholeness for the human being.

Our own experience teaches us that our intention of providing therapy for the dying must undergo a reorientation. Jung, growing older, wrote the following letter in reference to this:

> The dead are surely not to be pitied—they have so infinitely much more before them than we do . . . my compassion goes out to those who, in the darkness of the world, hemmed in by a narrow horizon and the blindness of ignorance, must follow the river of their days, fulfilling life's task, only to see their whole existence, which was once the present brimming with vitality, crumbling bit by bit and crashing into the abyss. This spectacle of old age would be unendurable did we not know that our psyche reaches into a region held captive neither by change not by limitation of place. In that form of being our birth is death and our death a birth. The scales of the whole hang balanced. (Jung 1972b, 568)

The process of dying begins at birth, biologically and psychologically. The main archetypal route-markers of a human life, such as birth, entering adulthood, marriage and death, contain qualities of leaving as well as arriving. So in accompanying the living, every therapy is also an accompanying of the dying, and vice versa!

For that very reason, Death—as the final culmination of human life—seems to me the noblest instructor of life. The dying seem to find access to those laws and patterns which extend far beyond our rational system. They share in the archetypal order directly, but, in the final analysis, the living are embedded within it, as well. The encounter with death or the dying can mean a chance for the living, insofar as they may question the absolute validity of our earthly criteria and come to a new understanding about life: "... we have centuries to fritter away! Why then this senseless hurry? ... (But) perhaps one has to be close to death to acquire the necessary freedom ..." (Jaffé 1962)

Those who will be touched by the numinosity of death will attain this freedom and be armed to accompany the dying, instead of leaving them alone in the knowledge they have attained.

> A man should be able to say he has done his best to form a conception of life after death, or to create some image of it—even if he must confess his failure. Not to have done so is a vital loss. For the question that is posed to him is the age-old heritage of humanity: an archetype, rich in secret life, which seeks to add itself to our own individual life in order to make it whole. Reason sets the boundaries far too narrowly for us, and would have us accept only the known ... and that too with limitations— and live in a known framework, just as if we were sure how far life actually extends. As a matter of fact, day after day we live far beyond the bounds of our consciousness; without our knowledge, the life of the unconscious is also going on within us. The more the critical reason dominates, the more impoverished life becomes, but the more of the unconscious and the more of myth we are capable of making conscious, the more of life we integrate. Overvalued reason has this in common with political absolutism: under its dominion the individual is paupered. (Jaffé 1963, 280)

In a world controlled by rational thought, threatening to cut us off from our ancient legacy, where medicine misconstrues illness as a flaw and death as an irritating blunder, we must find new ways of drawing attention to the meaning of death for life. The more imminent the experience of death, the greater the potential for change. Synchronistic happenings in the proximity of death intimate the constellation of archetypes from which the power for change arises.

We need ways to help those close to the dying but not able to cope with the event, ways to help them accompany the process of death. The pictorial statements of the dying as a wordless and therefore less-adulterated expression of the unconscious have proved to be a precious bridge to bring relatives nearer to the experience of dying, even allowing them to share in the transforming power of the images. Helpers, too, need help. An encounter with their own archetypal nature when painting or modelling, or during nature-play in the presence of one already initiated, enables a trust to develop in the numinous powers surrounding the dying.

It is not the glorification of death and contempt for life, but the real encounter and involvement of the living with death which contains within it the potential for a new and fruitful reorientation in this life.

With succinct clarity, Herzog (1960, 245) summed up the significance of death for the living:

> ... from death light falls on life—and only one ready in his soul to step through the gateway of death will then become a human being.

[The case studies of Elisabeth and Stefan are discussed more extensively in the book *Was kranke Kinder sagen wollen* (What Sick Children Want to Say) by Kaspar Kiepenheuer (Kreuz Verlag, 1989); the English translation is to be published in 1991 by Sigo Press, Boston.]

References

Bach, Susan. 1966. Spontanes Malen schwerkranker Patienten (Spontaneous Paintings of Seriously-Ill Patients). *Acta Psychosomatica,* 8. Basel (Geigy).

———. 1974/75. Spontaneous Pictures of Leucaemic Children as an Expression of the Total Personality, Mind and Body. *Acta Paedopsychiatrica,* 41, 86–104.

———. 1980. Guidelines for Reading and Evaluating Spontaneous Pictures. *Psychosomatische Medizin,* IX: 1/2, 5–14.

Eliade, M. 1958. *Birth and Rebirth.* New York: Harper and Row.

Evans-Wentz, W.Y. (ed.) 1971. *Das Tibetanische Totenbuch* (The Tibetan Book of the Dead). Olten: Walter.

Fierz, H.K. 1982. Das verlorene Symbol. In *Die Psychologie C.G. Jungs und die Psychiatrie.* Zurich: Daimon.

Hampe, J.C. 1975. *Sterben ist doch ganz anders.* Stuttgart: Kreuz-Verlag.

Herzog, E. 1960. Psyche und Tod. *Studienreihe des C.G. Jung-Institutes,* XI. Zurich: Rascher.

Hillman, J. 1966. *Selbstmord und seelische Wandlung* (Suicide and Spiritual Transformation). Zurich: Rascher.

Hitzig, W.H., and Kaspar Kiepenheuer. 1976. Das Kind und der Tod: Gedanken zur Beziehung zwischen Pädiater und todkranken Kind, *Hexagon 'Roche',* 4: 7, 1–10.

Jaffé, Aniela. 1962. *Erinnerungen, Träume, Gedanken von C.G. Jung.* surich: Rascher.

———. 1978. *Geisterscheinungen und Vorzeichen.* Olten: Walter.

———. 1980. Der Tod in der Sicht von C.G. Jung. In *Im Umkreis des Todes.* Zurich: Daimon.

Jung, C.G. 1952. Synchronizität als ein Prinzip akausaler Zusammenhänge. In *Naturerklarung und Psyche: Studien aus dem C.G. Jung-Institut.* Zurich: Rascher.

———. 1963. Zur Psychologie östlicher und westlicher Religionen. In *Collected Works* XI. Olten: Walter.

———. 1972a. *Briefe* (Letters) I. Olten: Walter.

———. 1972b. *Briefe* II. Olten: Walter.

———. 1973. *Briefe* III. Olten: Walter.

———. 1974. Zwei Schriften über Analytische Psychologie. In *Collected Works* VII. Olten: Walter.

_____. 1976a. Die Dynamik des Unbewußten. In *Collected Works* VIII. Olten: Walter.

_____. 1976b. Seele und Tod. In *Collected Works* VIII. Olten: Walter.

Kalff, Dora L. 1979. *Sandspiel.* Erlenbach/Zurich: Rentsch.

Kiepenheuer, Kaspar. 1978. Die innere Welt des sterbenden Kinders (The Inner World of Dying Children). *Familiendynamik,* 3: 4.

_____. 1980. Spontaneous Drawings of a Leukemic Child: An Aid for a More Comprehensive Care of Fatally Ill Children and their Families. *Psychosomatische Medezin,* IX: 1/2, 28–38.

_____. 1982. "Stirb und werde!" Zurich: Self-published.

_____. 1984. Stirb und werde! Archetypische Betrachtung einer Pubertätskrise. *Schweizer Archiv für Neurologie, Neurochirurgie, und Psychiatrie.* 134: 2.

Masereel, F. 1947. *Die Sonne.* Stuttgart: Recalm.

Moody, R. 1977. *Life after Life.* Covington, Ga: Mockingbird.

Wiesenhütter, E. 1978. *Grundfragen der Existenz.* Zurich: Kindler.

Index